Wonderfully Made

Girl Devotional for Ages 08 to 11

ADISAN Publishing AB

By

EILEEN NYBERG

Table of Contents

Introduction

Hi Girls! I am excited to talk about God with you. I think he's the most amazing, creative, kind God! You will see that each day as we read a bible verse and talk about it. How many bones are in the neck of a giraffe? How did God make fish? How can we be a good friend? What can we do when someone is mean to us? What can I do when I'm scared? Why do I feel alone? What can I do when I am mad? What does God want me to do today? We will talk about all these things and more! We will talk about Jesus and Jesus' ways. I can't wait to talk about our great God with you! You were made for him!

PART ONE

God is An Amazing Creator

1.Earth

Do you like to make cookies? Do you know how to make them? Did you ever make them with your mom or grandma? Not the frozen kind that you cut. I mean from scratch. That's the kind that is hard work. First, we get flour, right? We add eggs, milk, butter, sugar, chocolate chips. We stir all that to-gether. Are we done? Nope! We have to scoop that dough out and put it on a cookie sheet. Are we done? Not yet! We have to put the cookies in the oven and wait. Are we finished? Not quite! When they are done baking, we have to wait for them to cool. Finally, we get to try our cookies with a big glass of milk. Whew! That's a lot of work.

Do you know what's amazing about when God makes stuff? He makes it from nothing! Wow. In the Bible, it says that he just said the words, and it happened. He said, "Let the earth make plants." And do you know what happened? Trees, flow-ers, bushes, and vines all just immediately grew! I would have loved to see that happen, wouldn't you?

BEDTIME PRAYER

Dear God, You are great at making things! I am amazed at how powerful your words are!

2. Water

'Worship God. He made the heavens, the earth, the sea, and the springs of water. Revelation 14:7

Have you ever been to the beach? Or maybe you've seen it in a movie? The waves crash on the sand. Imagine squishing the sand in your toes and watching the waves. A small, warm breeze blows across your face. It feels good, doesn't it? It feels good to rest and watch God's beautiful waters. Have you ever swum in the ocean? If you have, then you know just how salty it is! There is a huge amount of ocean water on our earth. And, God made freshwater too. The rivers and lakes are not salty. God made it that way.

God made salty and fresh water. And, there are animals and plants that can ONLY live in one or the other. Let's think about that. God created different kinds of water for different kinds of animals. Isn't he smart? Only he could have done that!

* * * * *

BEDTIME PRAYER

Dear God, Thank you for making water. I am glad that we have water to drink and wash our hands and also play in. It was very smart of you to make water for all the plants and animals. I worship you. You are an amazing creator.

3. Sun

*It is good to be alive to enjoy the
light of day. Ecclesiastes 11:7*

Let's close our eyes for a minute and imagine that we are standing in the sun. Just close your eyes and take a couple of deep breaths. The sun is so warm, right? We can even turn our faces to the sun in winter and feel the warmth from it. I love sunglasses and sandals. I love shorts. I love snow cones on a hot summer day! The sun is huge. It's so much bigger than the earth - like WAY bigger.   But it's so far away - like SUPER far away. Because it's so far, it seems smaller to us. It's the perfect heater for the earth. It's the perfect source of light for plants and us.

It is really good for us to get a little sun every day. That's how our bodies make the vitamin D that we need. So when the Bible says it's good for us to enjoy the light of day, it really does mean it's good!

• • • • • •

BEDTIME PRAYER

Dear God, You had a great idea when you made the sun. Thank you for making it. I like to _______ in the sun! You think about everything we need!

4. Moon

You made the moon to mark the seasons. Psalm 104:19

My dad made a fire in our backyard. My brother and I helped him. Mom came out after a while and brought marshmallows. My favorite! We had a great time that night. When dad started the fine, it was still light. But, the longer we sat out there, the darker it got. Finally, it was dark. The fire was small. And do you know what we saw? A big, full moon! I couldn't believe it. It was so big and such a beautiful orange. My dad told me that it is called a Harvest Moon. The Harvest Moon comes at the beginning of fall - the season when farmers harvest their crops. Have you ever seen one? Maybe ask your mom or dad if they have seen one.

I love the moon. Sometimes it looks like a smile. Sometimes it looks like a half-circle. Sometimes I can see the "man in the moon." Do you like the moon? The Bible says that God made the moon to be the light for the nighttime. And, he gave it to us to help us "mark the seasons." Neat!

BEDTIME PRAYER

Dear God, Thank you for making the moon for us. Sometimes it feels like a bright night light. You thought of everything that we would need on earth. You are very great!

5. Stars

"Look up to the skies. Who created all these stars? ...He calls all the stars by name. He is very strong and full of power. So not one of them is missing." Isaiah 40:26

What is something that is hard to count? Can you count how many books you have? Probably. Can you count how many stuffed animals you have? Most likely. Can you count how much change your mom and dad have? Maybe, maybe not. Usually, we can count the things we have. But, do you know what we cannot count? The things that God has made. Just think about the stars for a minute. How many are there? More than we can count!

It's amazing to me that God created the stars. Then he named each of them. How does he remember all those names? Have you ever tried to count them and name them? God knows everything. The Bible says he even knows how many hairs are on your head. That's shocking! I have a lot of hair, and some come out every day! How many do I have today, Jesus?

BEDTIME PRAYER

Dear God, You are so smart! I'm shocked that you know all the stars by name. I am amazed that you can know everything. Help me remember how smart you are and to ask you for help. You always know the answer!

6. Earth Animals

*Then God said, 'Let the earth be filled
with animals.' Genesis 1:24*

Once I was driving in a big park. I saw an armadillo run across the road. I was so surprised! I had never seen one. Its short, little legs looked funny, running under its stiff body. One time, I helped hold a big snake at an animal show. And it was really big! It took 6 of us to hold it. Wow! It was so cool. I didn't know that I liked armadillos and snakes so much. I also love to pet our dog and our cat. I love to see them play or sleep. I can often see pretty butterflies in my garden. And I love to catch fireflies. God did a really great job making so many different kinds of animals to put on earth. Which is your favorite one?

God thought of so many different kinds of animals. Think for a minute about all the different kinds. Giraffes with their long necks. Kangaroos with their big feet. Penguins - birds that don't fly and love the cold. Let's think about it! He is so creative!

● ● ● ● ● ●

BEDTIME PRAYER

Dear God, Wow! You made really fun animals. I love what you created! Thanks for making ___________! It's my favorite animal that you made!

7. Sea Animals

Then God said, "Let the water be filled with living things. And let birds fly in the air above the earth." Genesis 1:20

Do you know what a baby dolphin is called? It's called a calf. They can't smell. But, they can see really well. They never sleep all the way either. They have to stay a little awake to come up for air. I think they are the cutest, friendliest animals in the ocean. What do you think? Which ocean animal do you like? Do you like big whales or tiny sea horses? Or maybe you like starfish or turtles? The ocean is full of amazing animals.

God made the ocean animals so different and fun. He said, "Let the water be **filled** with living things." And, it was. Did you know that the ocean has a lot of animals that we haven't even found yet? That's hard to imagine! God is more creative than we can know. And we already know he's creative! What animal do you think is the most creative?

- - - - -

BEDTIME PRAYER

Dear God, I think the oceans that you made are really amazing. You made so many different animals. You are so creative! I think the ___________ is the best. Thanks for making animals for me to see. You are so great!

8. Insects

*"So God made the wild animals, the tame animals,
and all the small crawling animals..." Genesis 1:25*

Do you love bugs or hate them? Some kids think they're awe-some. Some kids can't even look at them. Everyone is so different! I don't like to find them in my house. But, I really enjoy seeing them outside in their "house." One summer, we had a praying mantis in our yard. Its wing was broken, so it stayed around the same bushes. We found him every day. We would bring him other insects to eat. It was so fun to watch him grab the meal right from our hands!

Even if you don't really like bugs, you have to admit God showed off his creativity again! And they really help us. They help pollinate plants. They make honey. They also eat stinky stuff that we don't like - like leftover food, leaves, and twigs. Some bugs eat other bugs that are really bad for our plants. And, they can also be food for other bigger animals - the ones you might like better! God is a good planner!

* * * * * *

BEDTIME PRAYER

Dear God, You are very smart! I don't always like the bugs you made, but they are very helpful. Thank you for thinking of everything we need to make the world work well!

9. Birds

*"I know every bird in the mountains,
and the insects in the fields are mine."* Psalm 50:11

One time at the zoo, my youngest daughter stuck her hand out and gently felt the neck of a flamingo. The tall, pink bird was standing so close. It was right inside the fence that she was standing on. She just wanted to know what those feathers felt like. She said they were so soft! Of course, we told her that she couldn't do that. But, what a special bird that God made! He made a very tall, pink bird!

God made birds. He knows every kind of bird and what they eat. He knows where they fly and make a nest. Some make their nests on the ground. Some make their nests on the tree branches. Some dig a hole in the dirt or tree to make their safe place. Some birds are tall, like the ostrich. Some are small, like the hummingbird. Most birds can fly, but there are some who can't! All these birds remind us about how creative and powerful our God is. He made so many different kinds!

● ● ● ● ● ●

BEDTIME PRAYER

Dear God, Thank you for making birds. Help me to remember how creative and powerful you when I see birds. You are a great creator!

10. Weather

"God gives rain to the earth.
He sends water on the fields." Job 5:10

Last year we got a lot of snow for winter. And I mean, a lot! My girls built a big snow fort with a snow fence and a snow table. It was so fun. Sometimes when it rains, my youngest daughter loves to just go and roll down the driveway. She loves the feel of rain on her skin. My older daughter likes the sun. She wants to be at the pool every day in the summer. I like fall best. I like hiking in the woods with all the different colors on the trees.

The Bible says that God gave the weather. And it works really well. He waters the plants with rain. Snow helps the earth not get too hot. The sun gives light and warmth. Sometimes we may not be happy about the weather. It can rain when we wanted to play outside. It can be really windy and make us feel cold. But, we should remember that God gives us the weather for lots of reasons. He knows what is best for the earth and us!

BEDTIME PRAYER

Dear God, Thank you for making sure everything on earth works just right. Thank you for the rain, sun, and wind that remind me that you are taking care of us.

11. Rainbows

And God said, "I am making an agreement between me and you and every living creature that is with you. It will continue from now on. This is the sign: I am putting my rainbow in the clouds. It is the sign of the agreement between me and the earth." **Genesis 9:12-13**

Do you know the seven colors in a rainbow? When I was in 5th grade, my teacher taught me a way to remember them. If I could remember the name "Roy G. Biv," I could remember all the colors. **R**ed, **O**range, **Y**ellow, **G**reen, **B**lue, **I**ndigo, **V**iolet. I used to follow the rainbow as far as I could with my eyes. Then I would imagine a wonderful, magical place at the end.

Rainbows are wonderful things. Have you ever seen a double rainbow? I love those! God uses two things to make a rainbow - water and light.   And every time he makes one, it is to remind us about the first rainbow ever.   The Bible says that the first rainbow was a sign that God made a promise to the earth. He promised to never flood the entire earth again. He never has because he does not break his promises.

• • • • • •

BEDTIME PRAYER

Dear God, I am really glad you created rainbows. Help me remember that you are a God who never breaks your promise. I love you!

12. Clouds

*"If clouds are full of rain, they will pour
water on the earth." Ecclesiastes 3:11*

I remember when I was a kid. I sat on the porch with my mom.
There was a summer storm coming. The big gray clouds were
moving quickly. The wind started blowing stronger. And it
smelled like rain. Can you smell the rain when it is coming? I
also remember laying in the grass on a different summer day.
I watched the big, white clouds moving slowly. I could see
animals in them. I could see a horse, a crocodile mouth, and
a woman holding a baby. I could imagine different creatures
floating by. Sometimes I made stories up about them. Those
two experiences with clouds are very different. But I loved
them both. And I loved the clouds that God made.

God made the clouds a very special part of helping our earth.
There are many things that clouds do to help us. They give
water to the plants. Help keep us cooler. They even help
clean the water. God is really wise to make clouds to help us.

● ● ● ● ● ●

BEDTIME PRAYER

Dear God, You are a smart creator. Thank you for making
clouds to be a watering can for our flowers and food. I like
your Clouds!

PART TWO

You were made by God

13. Wonderfully Made

"You made my whole being. You formed me in my mother's body. I praise you because you made me in an amazing and wonderful way. What you have done is wonderful. I know this very well." Psalm 139:13-14

Did you ever make something really special for someone? Maybe you created a beautiful picture or a necklace with beads. Maybe you wrote a nice birthday card for someone. See if you can remember something. How did you feel when you made it? Sometimes when I make something, I feel proud. I worked hard, and I am happy with it. Sometimes when I make something, I feel mad. If it doesn't turn out the way I want, I can feel sad.

Psalm 139 says that God made you. And do you know what is so exciting about that? He is not sad or mad with this daughter he made! He knows that you are made in an amazing way. Everything He does is good.

God wants you to remember today that he did a great job when he made you! You are uniquely and wonderfully created by God.

• • • • •

BEDTIME PRAYER

Dear God, Thank you for making me just as you wanted. You thought about me and who I would be. Always help me remember that you made me and that you do a good job!

14. Amazing Life

*"The Spirit of God created me. The breath of
God All-Powerful gave me life." Job 33:4*

Have you ever sledded down a hill really fast? Or maybe you've ridden your bike down a hill and felt the wind in your face? One time I rode on a roller coaster. It was fast and fun. It was also a little scary. But, something about going fast makes me think about God's power. I can't go that fast without help. I need a sled or a bike or a roller coaster. And when I do go fast, I can feel the power in the speed.

The scripture today helps us think about the power of God. He created me. That's powerful! If I think for a minute about different special parts of our bodies, I am amazed. The eye is amazing. It takes in information upside down. Our brain is amazing because it flips the information right-side-up so we can understand it. Our heart is amazing because it never stops. It always beats even when I sleep. God made you and gave you life. Isn't he amazing?

● ● ● ● ● ●

BEDTIME PRAYER

Dear God, You are all-powerful! You made me and gave me life. Thank you for making my heart to keep beating!

15. Made in his image

"So God created human beings in his image. In the image of God, he created them." Genesis 1:27

At the children's museum, there are mirrors. They make me look silly. One makes me look super tall. One makes me look super fat. And one makes my body wavy. It's really fun to see. Have you ever done that? Or, maybe you have a filter on your phone. When you take a picture, can you put on ears? Or, can you put on a funny hat? I like the one that makes my mouth look really big.

It's fun to see an image of ourselves.   An image means that it's not us, but it is a picture of us. Or, it looks a lot like us. The Bible says that we were made in God's image. That means we are made to look like him. We aren't him, but we can remind people of him. We can look like him. Isn't that neat?! We can remind people about Jesus by the things that we say or the way we treat others. We also remind people of him when we talk about how great he is!

● ● ● ● ● ●

BEDTIME PRAYER

Dear God, Help me remember that I am made in your image. Help me to remind people about who you are. Thanks for making me like you! It's an important job.

16. Formed by His Hand

"But Lord, you are our father. We are like clay, and you are the potter. Your hands made us all." Isaiah 64:8

Have you ever made something out of playdough? Or have you used clay? In fourth grade, we made clay items. Some kids used a potter's wheel to make small cups. I didn't want to be a potter, so I made mine at my table. We painted them. The teacher heated them up. Then they were shiny. I looked for my heart when they were done. Where was it? I had made a beautiful heart bowl. I wanted to give it to my mom.

I looked again later. There were just 3 pieces left. One was a lopsided heart. The sides were squished up. It was pink and gray and messy. I turned it over. O my! It was my name on the bottom! I was shocked. I thought it was a disaster. But my mom didn't think so. She loved that heart bowl. She proudly put it on her dresser and kept her favorite earrings in it.

This scripture reminds us that we are like clay, and God forms us. He made us. He is happy with what he made! He is a perfect potter!

BEDTIME PRAYER

Dear God, Help me remember that you are a good potter! You made me just the way you wanted me!

17. Made for His glory

"Bring to me all the people who are mine. I made them for my glory. I formed them; I made them." Isaiah 43:7

Did you ever wonder why you're here right now in the place that you are? Why this family? Why this town? When I was younger, I moved five times. It was hard moving to a new house and new school. I had to make new friends. It was hard for me. I was kind of shy. But, you know what? I always made new friends. I always found a person or two that I called my best friends. I always found a place in my home and neighborhood.

Sometimes we can wonder why we are here. This verse reminds us that we were made for God's glory. What does that mean? It means you and I were made to declare how perfect and beautiful he is. We were formed by him so that we can tell others of his wonderful ways. I was made for that. YOU were made for that. It's an important reason - the most important reason - why we are in this place, at this time, with this family and these friends.

• • • • • • •

BEDTIME PRAYER

Dear God, Thanks for making me. It makes me feel good that you formed me. I want to tell others about your glory. You are worthy of my praise!

18. Made for a Special Job

*"Before I made you in your mother's womb, I chose you.
Before you were born, I set you apart for
a special work." Jeremiah 1:5*

What makes you special? What's something that is good about you? What do you like? Can you draw well? Can you be creative when you play? Do you like to cook? Do you help mom? Do you find great games? Are you a leader? Are you kind? Do you like animals? Are you strong? Do you like to color? Do you like to build?

There is nobody who is exactly like you. Today's scripture reminds us that God made us. And that's not all. He sets us apart. This scripture is said about Jeremiah specifically. He was a special helper to God. He helped speak God's truth. But, it's true about us too. We will talk more about this later but just think about it for a minute. He set Jeremiah apart for a special work. He has made you and set you apart for special work too! What's your special job today?

• • • • • •

BEDTIME PRAYER

Dear God, Thanks for making me and even giving me special work to help you. I know that you can do everything, but you still want me to help you. Thank you! I want to help. Please show me what to do tomorrow to help!

19. Made to Learn

"You made me and formed me with your hands. Give me understanding so I can learn your commands." Psalm 119:73

What's your favorite class? What's the most fun for you? Children usually say - RECESS. I loved recess too. I also liked English. I don't mean I always liked the work. But, I want English homework more than math homework any day. God gave us our interests. And he made us able to learn. Some classes are harder than others, though, right?

This scripture reminds us to pray and ask for understanding. He made us with the ability to learn. And we can ask for help!! The person who wrote this psalm said, "Give me understanding so I can learn your commands." God wants to help us learn about his ways and our math! Isn't it great that we can ask him for help?! He is a kind creator!

· · · · · ·

BEDTIME PRAYER

Dear God, Thanks for making me and giving me my mind. I think I am good at _______. Sometimes I have trouble with _______. Help me remember to ask for your help. I want to learn your ways!

20. Made for God's gifts

"Every good action and every perfect gift is from God. These good gifts come down from the Creator of the sun, moon, and stars. God does not change like their shifting shadows." James 1:17

We talked about how God is the creator of the world. We talked about how God is the creator of you and me. We talked about how he makes each of us special. He gives us special talents and gifts. He also gives us gifts. Sometimes you make a new friend, find a coin, feel especially happy. These are gifts from God. Sometimes you get ice cream, or pet your dog, or go swimming. These are also gifts from God. God has given us a lot of things that we can enjoy here on earth. These are part of his gifts.

Later we will talk about the best gift he ever gave to us. But today, let's stop and think about something good that happened today. Did you get to swing? Did you smile with a friend? Did you eat one of your favorite foods? Let's thank God today for that. He made us. He made that gift. And then, he gave it to you.

● ● ● ● ● ●

BEDTIME PRAYER

Dear God, Thanks for making me to enjoy your gifts. And thanks for giving gifts! Help me see all your gifts throughout the day.

21. Made to Give Gifts

"Each of you received a spiritual gift. God has shown you his grace in giving you different gifts." 1 Peter 4:10

My daughters are very different. One likes rules. Correction... She LOVES rules. The other one does not. She loves surprises. The first daughter likes art. The second one likes electronic games. One likes dogs, the other one likes cats. One is quiet and shy. The other one is loud and friendly. God has made us all different. He has given us each different giftings.

Some giftings are easy to see. Maybe you can play an instrument. Maybe you can jump rope well. God has given these interests to you. He has also given you spiritual gifts. Special ways that you, and only you, can show others his love. Some girls like to have friends over. That's a way to share the love. Some like to write a little note. That shares love. Maybe you like to help others, listen to someone when they are sad, or give hugs. We can use our giftings to show love to others.

● ● ● ● ● ●

BEDTIME PRAYER

Dear God, You made me just the way I am. And you gave me gifts - spiritual gifts - so that I can show others how great you are. Thank you for giving me gifts!

22. It was Good

"God looked at everything he had made,
and it was very good." Genesis 1:31

God made everything that we can see and everything that we cannot see in 6 days. You probably remember from an earlier devotion that he made everything from nothing. He just spoke, and it was created. On day one, God made light. He called the light day. On day two, he made the sky and the oceans. Day three, he spoke for the land to make with all the plants. On day four, he created the sun and moon, and stars. It was day five, and he made all the birds and all the animals that live in the sea. Finally, he made land animals and people. And when he was all done, he saw that it was all very good.

God is very pleased with the things he makes - including you. God is very pleased that he made you. He does a good job of making people. You are a special part of his creation. Creating you was a part of all that is very good.

BEDTIME PRAYER

Dear God, You are good at what you do. When I think about how you made me, I feel happy. I am happy to know that you thought of me and made me.

23. Made for Right Now

"God began by making one man. From him came all the different people who live everywhere in the world. He decided exactly when and where they must live. "Acts 17:26

What would it be like to live a hundred years ago? Do you know much about the time that long ago? Would you have a cell phone? Would you have your car? What did children do all day a hundred years ago? Did they watch movies? Did they order toys off the Internet?

Who decided that you would live during this time and not a hundred years ago? God did!   God decided that you and I would be born now and not so long ago. He decided what country we would live in. Maybe sometimes you don't like all his decisions, but he knows what he is doing. Do you remember how we talked about how he created everything from nothing? Do you remember how he knows all the stars' names? He is very smart. He knows everything! He even knows why he put us here at this time. We can trust him!

• • • • • •

BEDTIME PRAYER

Dear God, You are very powerful because you make everything. You are very wise because you know everything. You know all the reasons why I live at this place at this time. Help me to trust you when I don't understand something.

24. Thank you!

"Our Lord and God! You are worthy to receive glory and honor and power. You made all things. Everything existed and was made because you wanted it." Revelation 4:11

Have you ever gotten something that you really wanted? Did you ever dream about a toy or a trip or a phone? And then one day, did that dream come true? It's an amazing feeling. I wanted a big, beautiful glass doll for my 10th birthday. Her name was Olivia. She had curly, light brown hair. She had a sweet dress with little flowers. She had a stand that held her up. I saw her in a magazine, and I begged my mom for it. I didn't get it for my birthday.

But I did get it for Christmas months later! Can you imagine how happy I was? What do you think I did first? I yelled, "Thank you!" to my mom. And I gave her a big hug. I loved and cared for that doll for a long time. But many times, I thought about how my mom gave it to me.

God created a very beautiful world. He made a very beautiful girl - YOU! He gave us life and this world. And we can remember to say, "Thank you!" to him.

● ● ● ● ●

BEDTIME PRAYER

Dear God, Thank you for my life and this world! You are very kind!

PART THREE

You were made
for a relationship
with God

25. Singing

*"The Lord your God is with you. The mighty One will save you.
The Lord will be happy with you. You will rest in his love.
He will sing and be joyful about you." Zephaniah 3:17*

Can you imagine God singing and being joyful about you?
GOD. The one who created everything. He spoke, and light
erupted. He said it, then animals showed up. This is a powerful, mighty God. He knew what every plant, animal, and
person would need to live. This is wise God. The God who
thought about you and planned you and your life. This is a
fatherly God. And this God is joyful about YOU and me.

Let's think about those words for a moment. And let it wrap
you up like a warm blanket or a gentle hug. Let this truth
about God enjoying you fill you with his love. He is thinking
about you. He is right with us. We are going to talk more
about this and see how to walk with him. He is our father.

● ● ● ● ● ●

BEDTIME PRAYER

Dear God, When I think about you thinking about me, I feel
happy. When I think about you feeling joyful about me, I feel
joyful too. Thank you for loving me! I love you too!

26. Forgiven

"All people have sinned and are not good enough for God's glory." **Romans 3:23.**

We all mess up, don't we?   One time I took a piece of candy from my neighbor's house. She was on vacation. She paid me to feed her cats while they were gone. I fed the cats. The candy dish was right there, and I just grabbed it. It tasted good for a minute. But it felt wrong for a long time.   I don't know how my mom knew, but she did. When the neighbor lady got home, I had to call to tell her what I did and say sorry.

We all do things that are wrong. It's called sin. It keeps us far away from God because the Bible says he is perfect. But, guess what God did? Romans 5:8 says - *But Christ died for us while we were still sinners. In this way, God shows his great love for us.* I bet you know all about this! It's good to remember how we mess up every day and how God made way for us to be forgiven! Isn't our God amazing? He knows we can't be perfect. So Jesus lived the perfect life and died for our sins. Thanks, God!

• • • • •

BEDTIME PRAYER

Dear God, You are a kind and loving God to forgive my sins! Thank you!

27. Generous

"This is how God showed his love to us: He sent his only Son into the world to give us life through him." 1 John 4:9

Did you ever have only one of something? I had one piece of gum. My brother wanted it. I looked at that piece of big, yummy, sweet gum. And I said, "No. Next time." I wanted that gum. It was good gum! I had bought it with my own money. If I had two pieces, then I would have shared them. What would you have done?

I didn't know God then. I didn't know his ways of being generous. I didn't know how to love like that. Now I wish I would have given it to my brother. I would have been showing Jesus then. God showed his love for us by sending his ONLY son. He only had one. But he loved us and wanted us to be forgiven. Jesus loved us and died for us. Wow! This is amazing! He is a giver. He wants to be close with us and made a way! You were made for a relationship with God! Do you know John 3:16? Read it tomorrow. You'll love it!

BEDTIME PRAYER

Dear God, Thanks for showing me what it looks like to be generous. I'm amazed by your kindness! Thank you for loving me so much!

28. Growing

"I am the vine, and you are the branches. If a person remains in me and I remain in him, then he produces much fruit. But without me, he can do nothing." John 15:5

Where do you like to hang out? What's a good place for you to be by yourself? In your treehouse? In your room? Outside on a swing? Think about your favorite place to be. Can you imagine yourself there? I have a special chair in our office. There are lots of books. And I like my comfy chair. It's my favorite place to be alone.

When Jesus said this verse, it makes me think about my comfy chair. To remain in him means to hang out with him. We hang out with him by reading the Bible and praying. We can read our devotions too. Do you know what's great about being with God in this way? Jesus said that we grow. We can grow to be more loving and kinder. We can grow to know him better. We can grow to be more like him. You were made to walk with God. You were made to grow in his ways.

When you are in your favorite place, talk to God about your thoughts. You were made for a relationship with him!

● ● ● ● ●

BEDTIME PRAYER

Dear God, Thank you for helping me to grow in you today!

29. Peace

"You, Lord, give true peace. You give peace to those who depend on you. You give peace to those who trust you. So, trust the Lord always. Trust the Lord because he is our Rock forever. "Isaiah 26:3-4

We went to the children's museum. There was a special program that we were going to see. We met as a big group in the lobby. Then the guide led us right past the gate. We got to pass right by all the people waiting to pay. They were waiting to get their tickets. We went right past! We felt special.

Walking with God is really special too! He is very kind and helpful to us. One thing he likes to do to help his people is to give peace. Peace means feeling calm on the inside. Sometimes life feels really crazy. But God can give us peace inside. So we can ask him for his help. We practice trusting him. And he gives us peace.

Is there something today that you don't have peace about? An answer you need? A friendship that is not good right now? Was school hard? He will give peace to those who trust him. Try it right now!

• • • • •

BEDTIME PRAYER

Dear God, Help me to trust you about __________. Can you help me to remember that you can help me? Thank you for your peace!

30. Don't Fear

"Be strong and brave. Don't be afraid of them. Don't be frightened. The Lord your God will go with you. He will not leave you or forget you." Deuteronomy 31:6

Have you ever been afraid? I think most kids are. I know I was! Do you remember when Jesus and his men were in the boat, and the storm came? Do you remember how they felt? They felt scared! I would be too! Jesus was asleep. That's surprising, isn't it? There was a big storm. And Jesus is snoozing away.

What did the men do? They woke up Jesus! And Jesus helped them. He made the storm stop. We were made to have a relationship with God. We were made to need his help. It is good that we can ask him for his help when we need it. He wants us to! You know, he knows that children are especially good at asking for help. That's why in the book of Matthew, he told people listening to be more like children! Children often know they need help. Do you know when you need help? What do you do?

I hope you ask your parents for help. And I hope you know you can ask God for his help too!

• • • • •

BEDTIME PRAYER

Dear God, Thanks for making me for a relationship with you. I am so happy that you are here!

31. Children

"The Father has loved us so much! He loved us so much that we are called children of God. And we really are his children. But the people in the world do not understand that we are God's children, because they have not known him." 1 John 3:1

Did you ever daydream about being a princess or a movie star? When I was young, I sure did! I loved the dream of having a lot of money. I wanted a horse. And I wanted beautiful dresses. I wanted a big house. What do you wish for sometimes?

Something happened that was way better than becoming a princess or movie star. I learned about God. And then I learned that I could be his kid! That is way better than being a princess. Remember all the amazing things God did? He made the world. He made us. He loves us and forgives us. He gives us peace. This is the king of the world. Now we are his children. He is our dad! That's amazing!

BEDTIME PRAYER

Dear God, Thank you for making me your child. Thank you for helping me know about you and walk with you. You are a good dad!

32. My Dad

"And you are God's children. That is why God sent the Spirit of his Son into your hearts. The Spirit cries out, "Father, dear Father." Galatians 4:6

I named him Max. He was a big dog that just showed up in our yard. He didn't have a collar. He loved the food I shared with him. He came with me all around the yard. My dad made a fire that night, and Max sat with us. He ate our hot dogs. He let us pet him. I just had him for that one day, but he felt like mine. He was gone the next day, but my heart still felt like he was mine.

Do you know that feeling? When you feel like something or someone is yours? Maybe you have a special pet or a special toy. Maybe someone in your family feels special to you. That's what this verse is saying. It's saying that we can have that feeling in our hearts that God is MY dad. It's a really special thing to be God's kid. And it's a really special thing to have God as your dad. You were made to have this special relationship with God.

- - - - - -

BEDTIME PRAYER

Dear God, Thank you for teaching me about yourself. You are a kind dad! I am happy to be your child.

33. My People

*"I will walk with you and be your God.
And you will be my people." Leviticus 26:12*

I moved several times when I was young. New city. New house. New school. New friends. It was always hard for me. I am a little shy. "Going to a new school was the hardest thing for me. I never knew if I could find a new friend. The first day was always the scariest. Would I find someone who would like me and I would like them? Would they like dogs and music like me? Would they think I was nice enough?

It's really exciting when we understanding who walks with us. God said that he is our friend. In this verse, he uses the word "people." He says, "You will be my people." That's a good feeling. I went to a new school and wanted to find my friends - my "people." But, I already belonged to a "people" - God's people. And I already had a friend at the new school before I ever went. Jesus came with me! He was always my first friend at a new school. We were made for a friendship with Jesus!

BEDTIME PRAYER

Dear God, Thank you for being my friend. Thank you for reminding me that you are with me all the time. I feel happy to know you!

34. Know Him

"Then you will call my name. You will come to me and pray to me. And I will listen to you. You will search for me. And when you search for me with all your heart, you will find me!" Jeremiah 29:12-13

Who is the coolest person you know? Who would you love to meet someday? Do you want to meet the president? An inventor? Do you want to meet a person from the movies? Do you want to meet a singer? Sometimes we get to meet someone famous, but not usually. We can know about them. We can read about them. Or watch a video about them. But they don't know about us.

Here's something cool: God wants you to know him! God! The one who created everything and knows everything! God gave us the Bible to learn about him. He gave us his son so we can be forgiven and see someone who looks like him. God gave us the Holy Spirit to help us in many ways. But, I think it's so amazing that God wants us to know him, and he knows us.

We were made for a relationship with him!

● ● ● ● ● ●

BEDTIME PRAYER

Dear God, Thank you for listening to me when I pray. I love you! I am glad I know you!

35. Grace

"I mean that you have been saved by grace because you believe. You did not save yourselves. It was a gift from God. You cannot brag that you are saved by the work you have done." Ephesians 2:10

Did you ever read about the Tower of Babel? It's when men wanted to build a tower all the way up to heaven - by themselves. They wanted to make themselves famous without God. There are many things that we like to do by ourselves. We don't want help. We don't want ideas. We just want to do it. When my daughters were little, they said, "Me do it." They pushed my hand away and tried on their own.

But we can't save ourselves. We can't brag about saving ourselves by working hard. We can't be perfect like Jesus. We can't stop the sin in our hearts by ourselves. That's why God did it. The Bible calls this grace. He gave us the gift of forgiveness. He did it because he wants a relationship with us. That's what we were made for.

● ● ● ● ● ●

BEDTIME PRAYER

Dear God, Thanks for this gift of grace! Thank you for helping me because I cannot save myself. I am so glad I know you!

36. Come Near

"Come near to God, and God will come near to you." James 4:9

It's easy to do something wrong. One time I broke my friend's toy. It was a really cool bow. It was silver and plastic, but it really shot toy arrows. I loved it. And I broke it. I didn't mean to. His mom was mad at me. I felt very sad and mad. I didn't want to break it. It just happened. I just pulled back to shoot the arrow, and it broke.

Sometimes we do something wrong against God. When we sin, it's like we walk away from him a little bit. But the Bible says to just walk towards him. We've already talked a lot about his gift of forgiving us. He is very kind. 1 John 1:9 says, "But if we confess our sins, he will forgive our sins. We can trust God. He does what is right. He will make us clean from all the wrongs we have done." We can tell him we are sorry, and he forgives us, just like that.

He made us for a relationship with him! He always wants to forgive us!

● ● ● ● ● ●

BEDTIME PRAYER

Dear God, Thank you for being very kind to me. You make it easy for me to walk towards you. I love you!

PART FOUR

You were made for a relationship with others

37. Two are Better

"Two people are better than one. They get more done by working together. If one person falls, the other can help him up. But it is bad for the person who is alone when he falls. No one is there to help him. " Ecclesiastes 4:9-10

Do you like to have a lot of friends? Or do you like a few good ones? Or maybe you like to have just one really special friend. What makes you feel happiest? God made us with a need to have friends. We want them, AND we need them.

The Bible says that two people are better than one. Why? Because we can help each other. We can look out for each other. There are a lot of things that we can do on our own. But it's not always best that we do it on our own.

What do you like to do with friends? In what ways do you help each other? Do you look out for each other? With my friends, we helped each other on the playground. We made sure that none of our friends were alone. We shared our candy and food with each other. Do you do that too sometimes?

BEDTIME PRAYER

Dear God, Thanks for making me to have friends. I like to have friends. It makes me happy to think about my friend ___________.

38. Live in Peace

*"It is good and pleasant when God's people
live together in peace!" Psalm 133:1*

Did you ever have a fight with your friend? Or maybe with your brother or sister? My brother and I got mad at each other a lot. We always wanted to play different games. We always wanted to do things our own way. We always thought our way was best. Sometimes we had a lot of fun together. And sometimes, we did not.

This verse reminds us that it feels good when we get along with others. Sometimes it can be really hard. My brother sometimes didn't care about my idea or how I felt. I was older and could have helped. But I didn't want to. We can ask God to help us live together in peace! God can help us be kind. It will feel so good and pleasant!

He made us for relationship. So when we have good friend-ships, we feel good inside too!

● ● ● ● ●

BEDTIME PRAYER

Dear God, Thank you for my friends and my family! I'm sorry that sometimes I don't live in peace with them. Can you help me do that? Thank you for bringing peace.

39. Two Ears

"My dear brothers, always be willing to listen and slow to speak. Do not become angry easily. Anger will not help you live a good life as God wants." James 1:19-20

I broke my toy, and I was very mad. My mom didn't listen to me. My brother was mean. My dad was busy. Grrr! No one cared about my problems. Nobody listened to me. Then I told my mom," You won't listen to me!" I yelled it at her, real loud. My mom spoke really softly. She said, "It's hard to listen to someone so loud. It hurts my ears."

Hm... She said that I have to listen too. I have to hear what she wants to say. She was telling me about this verse! She said that God gave me two ears and only one mouth. I guess that means I needed to listen more! Then she said she would fix my toy when she was done with her job. Thanks, Mom!

God wants us to have good friendships. He made us for relationships with people.

• • • • • •

BEDTIME PRAYER

Dear God, Help me to think about listening to my friends and family. Help me be a good friend by not getting angry too fast. Thanks for always listening to me! I love you!

40. Humble

"Always be humble and gentle. Be patient and accept each other with love… Let peace hold you together." Ephesians 4:2-3

Do you know what humble means? It means - knowing that you are wrong sometimes. Everybody is wrong sometimes. Even me and you. When we can say that we are wrong, then we are humble. And that's a good thing!

There was a man in the Bible. He was a rich man. He was a famous man. He was the boss of an army! But he had a sickness that was all over his body. So he asked a man named Elisha what to do. Elisha knew God. The man said he needed to go get in the river. But the river was so dirty. The famous man did not want to get in that dirty river.

But he had a nice friend. His friend said to listen to the man who knew God. And do you know what? He did it. He got in that dirty river. And God healed him! He told Elisha that he was sorry for not trusting him and God.

It's good to say when we are wrong! It helps us build good relationships with our friends!

BEDTIME PRAYER

Dear God, I know you want me to be a good friend. Thank you for helping me to say when I'm wrong.

41. Parents

"Children, obey your parents the way the Lord wants. This is the right thing to do. The command says, "Honor your father and mother." This is the first command that has a promise with it. The promise is: "Then everything will be well with you, and you will have a long life on the earth." Ephesians 6:1-3

Parents are really special. They are like a boss to us. They are like a friend to us. They help us a lot. They make good food. They keep us safe. We can feel really happy about that. Sometimes we can feel not so happy. I like to be a boss too. I have ideas too.

But God tells children to listen to mom and dad. He says he will even help us with our life when we listen to them. It must be really important to God. He tells parents to love us and take care of us. He tells us to love our mom and dad and listen to them. It's because we are made for relationships. Our heart is happy when we have good friendships with mom and dad!

● ● ● ● ● ●

BEDTIME PRAYER

Dear God, Thanks for my parents! Thank you for my grandparents. Help me to listen well. I love them and want to have good friendships with them! I also know this makes you and me both feel happy!

42. Made for Friends

"Then the Lord God said, "It is not good for the man to be alone. I will make a helper who is right for him." Genesis 2:18

I love my dog. She is smart. She is funny. She is mostly good. She makes me feel happy when I pet her or play with her. I laugh when my children play chase with her. She is a great dog. We found her at the shelter, and her eyes said, "I'm yours." So we took her home. And she is ours.

But, she is not a good helper sometimes. She does lots of tricks. But, she doesn't wash dishes or folds clothes. She only picks up her toys when we make her. God made us to be friends with dogs (and other animals!), but he made us to be friends with people most of all.

God made Adam. He knew Adam needed to have a friend. The Bible says that God showed all the animals to Adam. Adam named them. And when they did that big job, they looked around. There were no really good helpers.

So God made Eve. We were made for friendships! We were made to help each other.

• • • • • •

BEDTIME PRAYER

Dear God, Thank you for thinking about everything we need. You are very smart.

43. Wrong Word

*"So comfort each other and give each other strength,
just as you are doing now. " 1 Thessalonians 5:11*

One time I said the wrong word. I was in a play at school. Right in the middle of the stage. I wanted to say, "Stop the show!" I was supposed to say that. But what came out of my mouth was, "Stop the floor!" Why did I say that?! I don't know. The parents laughed. And my face was red. I felt sad. I didn't want to be funny. I wanted to say it right.

I was still sad after the show. My friend came over and sat by me. She told me that when I said that it was the best part of the show. She said she liked the surprise. I felt a little better. You know what? My mom said it was the best show of her life.

This verse tells us to help each other with our words. Our words are important. We can help our friends feel better. Sometimes things in life are hard. Sometimes things go wrong. But we can share important words with our friends. We were made for relationships with people!

* * * * * *

BEDTIME PRAYER

Dear God, Thank you for giving me friends to help me when I feel sad. That is very kind of you! I want to do that too!

44. Bad Times, Good Times

"A friend loves you all the time. A brother is always there to help you in hard times." Proverbs 17:17

We have good days and bad days, don't we? Some days are happy days with our friends. Maybe some days are hard days. Do you know about Jesus and Peter in the Bible? They were good friends. They were very different. They had fun times. They had hard times. But, they were good friends. They helped each other.

One time Jesus felt sad. And Peter stood up to a bully for his friend, Jesus. One time Peter lied about being friends with Jesus. He didn't want to get in trouble. But Jesus loved Peter. He forgave Peter and helped him.

We can be good friends too. We can try and love all the time. We can always try to help. And our good friends will do that for us too. God made us for friendships!

BEDTIME PRAYER

Dear God, Help me to always try to love and help my friends. Thank you for giving me friends who can love and help me too. And thank you for the best friend of all, Jesus! He is the perfect friend!

45. Everyone Come

"Let the little children come to me. Don't stop them. The kingdom of God belongs to people who are like these little children."
Mark 10:13-14

Jesus is important. His friends know this. They know he has a big job to do. They know he is busy. So they wanted to help. They think there are too many people. So they tell the moms and dads to stop bringing their small children to Jesus.

Jesus wasn't happy about that. He wanted everyone to come. Jesus often looked for the people who were left out. He went to them. He liked them.

Jesus wants us to be like this too. He wants us to look for people who are alone. The ones that other people think are not important. He wants us to be good friends with them. Can you think of someone who needs a friend? Do you see someone who is often alone? Can you be like Jesus and be friends with them?

● ● ● ● ● ●

BEDTIME PRAYER

Dear God, Help me be like Jesus and find the ones who need friends. Help me be like you!

46. Not Perfect

*"Don't make friends with someone who easily gets angry...
If you do, you may learn to be like him."* **Proverbs 22:24-25**

Did you ever put food coloring in water? I love to make the water blue. One time I put a flower in the blue water. Do you know what happened? The white flower turned blue! The water changed the flower. It's fun to do. Maybe you can try it.

When the flower changed colors, I thought about this verse. God wants us to have good friends. Good friends are not perfect. But good friends are trying to be good friends. Good friends try to help. Good friends try to love. We learn to be good friends.

God wants us to BE good friends and to HAVE good friends. If someone is mad all the time, we can start to feel mad too. If someone is mean all the time, we can start to say mean things too.

We can be nice to everyone. But our close friends, our good friends, should want to be good friends to us too. We were made for friendships!

BEDTIME PRAYER

Dear God, Please help me to be a good friend. Please help me to make good friends. Thank you for being my best friend!

47. New King

"Jonathan made a promise to David. He did this because he loved David as much as himself." 1 Samuel 18:3

In the Bible, there are two good friends. One friend was Jonathan. And one was David. Jonathan was the king's son. So who is the next king? Everyone knows - Jonathan. Right? No! God said David is the next king. Wow! What if that was you? Do you want David to be king?

The king's son may feel mad at God. Why does God want David to be king?! But Jonathan isn't mad. He loved David. He loved him very much. So, he helped David. He helped David stay safe. He helped David be the new king.

Friends always help. They love and help each other. Even when God says they're the next king. It's hard to do. But that's a good friend!

We were made to love friends!

BEDTIME PRAYER

Dear God, Thanks for telling me about these friends. I want to be a good friend too. I want to help my friends. I want to love my friends. Help me learn to do this.

48. Happy and Sad

"Be happy with those who are happy. Be sad with those who are sad." Romans 12:15

What things make us feel happy? Birthday cake? Doggy kisses? Winning a race? Swimming? Jesus? What kind of things make us feel sad? Sickness? Fights with friends? Getting hurt? Sin? We have a lot of feelings. God made us with lots of different feelings. We can feel happy and sad. We can feel mad and hurt. We can feel frustrated. We can feel scared. Sometimes we feel surprised.

This Bible verse is telling us how to be a good friend. If your friend is happy, be happy with them. If your friend is sad, be sad with them. Why is this being a good friend?

If you did a great job at school and got an A, you would be happy. Right? Let's say you showed your friend. What if she pushed your paper away? Maybe she said, "O, well, I got an A+!" How would that feel?

God is smart to tell us how to be good friends. It feels good to share these feelings with friends. If our friend gets an A+, we can feel happy with her! And if we get an A, she can feel happy with us! We were made for friendships!

• • • • • •

BEDTIME PRAYER

Dear God, Thanks for teaching me how to be a good friend!

PART FIVE

You were made for good works

49. The Plan

"God has made us what we are. In Christ Jesus, God made us new people so that we would do good works. God had planned in advance those good works for us. He had planned for us to live our lives doing them." Ephesians 2:10

God has made us for a special job. Did you know that? Did you know that God has something for us to do? He made us to do good works. What does that mean?

Good works help others see Jesus. Good works help show how good and kind God is. We were made to tell others about him. One way we do that is by doing good works. The Bible says he planned it for us. And we all know he is a good planner! He did a great job creating the world. He did a great job making us. He knows what he is doing.

We are going to talk more about these special jobs called "good works." Do you have any ideas about what things you can do? What can you do to show others how good God is?

BEDTIME PRAYER

Dear God, Thank you for planning my life. Thank you for planning out good things for me to do to help others. Help me know what to do. I love you!

50. Sharing

"Every animal of the forest is already mine. The cattle on a thousand hills are mine. I know every bird on the mountains. Every living thing in the fields is mine." Psalm 50:10-11

His name was George. He was my bird. He was blue and white and beautiful. George lived in my room when I was 9 because he was my bird. He was noisy and messy. He also liked to bite. Ouch! But he was mine. I made my brother mad many times because I wouldn't share George. My brother wasn't allowed to touch him because he belonged to me. I was the boss of George.

God is the boss of this world. He is the king of all creation. Everything that we can see and everything that we can't see belongs to him. He made it, so it's his. Because he is king, he can choose to do whatever he wants. He could keep it all to himself like I did, George. But he wants to share. He is a kind king! I want to be like him!

• • • • • •

BEDTIME PRAYER

Dear God, Thank you for sharing your world with me. I know it all belongs to you, but I really enjoy seeing it and using it. Thank you for being such a nice king!

51. Gifts

"Each of you received a spiritual gift. God has shown you his grace in giving you different gifts... use your gifts to serve each other." 1 Peter 4:10

Think of someone you really look up to. What do you like about them? I really look up to my aunt. She is creative and very sweet. Now think of something that you really like about yourself. This can be really hard for some people. But there are many wonderful things about you! What is something that you like? I like that I can be calm and quiet. I like feeling peaceful.

God made us what we are. He made my aunt creative. She paints pretty pictures. He made my dad smart about fixing things. I think he can fix almost anything. He made me calm. I don't yell or get upset about a lot of things because I like to be calm.

God made us the way we are, so we can share it. He wants us to show others how great he is. We can do this by using the gifts God gives us. What are you good at already? What are you getting better at? What can you do to love others with this gift?

• • • • • •

BEDTIME PRAYER

Dear God, Thank you for giving me gifts. I know you want me to share them. Please help me do that!!

52. Who Needs Help?

"My children, our love should not be only words and talk. Our love must be true love. And we should show that love by what we do." 1 John 3:18

The Bible talks a lot about helping others. When Jesus came, he showed us what God the Father likes. God likes it when we love. He likes it when we take care of others. There are lots of stories in the Bible about this. Maybe you know this one...

There was a man who got hurt. Some bad men hurt him. And nobody wanted to help him. They left him hurting on the road. But there was a kind man who came by. He helped him. He took care of him and took him to a hotel. He paid for the hurt man to stay at this hotel until he was better. It cost a lot of money to do that!

After Jesus told that story, he said that we should do the same thing. You probably don't see people like that, but maybe you see someone at school who needs help. Is there a kid who doesn't have many friends? Is there someone feeling sad that you can share God's love with?

God wants us to not just say we love others but to show we love others.

• • • • • •

BEDTIME PRAYER

Dear God, Help me show your love tomorrow.

53. Love the Hard to Love

"You are God's children whom he loves. So try to be like God. Live a life of love. Love other people just as Christ loved us."
Ephesians 5:1-2

There was a man who nobody liked. He worked getting taxes from people. And he wasn't nice about it. Nobody wanted to be his friend. Nobody felt bad for him. Everyone was mad at him. But he wanted to see Jesus. He heard that Jesus was different. So he went to see Jesus. When Jesus walked by, he stopped and looked right at the man. The man who nobody liked. He said he wanted to hang out with him. That surprised everyone!

Sometimes the Bible surprises us. Jesus is very different from us. He wants to teach us how to be like him. Why? Because he wants the world to know about his love. Jesus showed us that we can love people who are hard to love. Do you know anyone who is hard to love? Maybe it's someone at school or in your neighborhood? Sometimes it's hard to love our families. (Do remember any stories about my brother??) But Jesus can help us learn to live a life of love. We can love as Jesus did.

BEDTIME PRAYER

Dear God, Thank you for loving me. Thank you for showing me what love looks like. I love you!

54. Thinking of Others

"I feel sorry for these people. They have been with me for three days, and now they have nothing to eat. I don't want to send them away hungry. They might faint while going home." Mathew 15:32

Do you have a pet? If you don't, you can pretend you have one. Think about your pet. Think about all the ways that you help your pet. How do you take care of a pet? It always needs food. It always needs water, right? What else does it need? Does your pet like to play? Does your pet get lonely? When we love someone or something like a pet, we care about it. We try to take care of what it needs, right?

Jesus was thinking about this too. There were people with Jesus. A crowd of people was with him. They followed him for days. He knows they might be out of food. He knows they are probably hungry. He is thinking about what they need. We can ask Jesus to help us. We can learn to think about other people's needs too. We were made for good works!

● ● ● ● ● ●

BEDTIME PRAYER

Dear God, Thank you for caring about me. Please help me learn to care about others more and more. I want to be like you!

55. Open Hands

"There might be a poor man among you. Do not be selfish or greedy toward your poor brother. But give freely to him. Freely lend him whatever he needs." Deuteronomy 15:7-8

Imagine that you have something in your hand. Let's pretend it is really special. Let's pretend it's something important to you. Do you have something in mind? I am pretending I have my very special ring. It's pretty. It's special. What can you do so that I don't take your special thing from you? What can I do so that you can't take my special thing from me?

We can close our hands, right? We can close our fingers real tight. We can use all our power to keep our hands shut.

This verse reminds us of how God wants us to think. He wants us to keep our hands open. He wants us to take care of each other. This is a good work! We were made for good works! When we have our hands open, we share. We can be happy to give to others. We can share our toys, our food, our money, our time to help others. Sometimes it's hard, but God can help us do this.

• • • • • •

BEDTIME PRAYER

Dear God, Help me to remember how much you have given me. Please help me be good at sharing it.

56. Be Light

"You are the light that gives light to the world. A city that is built on a hill cannot be hidden. Live so that they will see the good things you do. Live so that they will praise your Father in heaven." Matthew 5:16

Have you ever sat in the dark? One time I went to a cave with our youth group. We had to walk down first. The air was cool. The light got smaller and smaller. Then we had to crawl and squeeze through different places. We all had flashlights. But at one place, it was an opening - like a room - and we all turned off our flashlights. It was total darkness. I couldn't see my hand in front of my face. Wow!

That's like this world. It's dark because of sin. Jesus is the light. And we can show him to the world by what we say and do. It's like turning the flashlight on in that cave. The light looked so bright! Our good works show Jesus' brightness.

BEDTIME PRAYER

Dear God, Help me show you as the light by what I say and do tomorrow.

57. Get Ready

"Using the Scriptures, the person who serves God will be ready and will have everything he needs to do every good work." 2 Timothy 3:17

The Bible is our teacher. It shows us who God is. It explains who Jesus is. It shows us God's ways. This scripture reminds us that we can use the Bible to get ready. The Bible helps us get ready to do every good work.

How can the Bible help us to get ready? Well, there are many stories that we can see God's ways. There are many stories when we can see how Jesus loves people. Let's think of some...Jesus helped his friends catch fish. (Luke 5) He stopped the storm. (Matthew 8) Fed a lot of people. (John 6) He healed a blind man. (John 9) He washed his friends' feet. (John 13) He healed a very sick 12-year-old girl. (Luke 8) The Bible is full of examples of how to love. We try to be like Jesus. We can help the sick and the hungry. We can help our friends with their chores. We can be good friends with everyone. That's good works!

• • • • • •

BEDTIME PRAYER

Dear God, Thank you for the Bible. Help me to read it and obey it. I am happy that I can know you more when I read it!

58. Powerful Words

"When you talk, do not say harmful things. But say what people need—words that will help others become stronger. Then what you say will help those who listen to you." Ephesians 4:29

Our words are very powerful, aren't they? Can you think of the nicest thing someone ever said to you? What do you love to hear from your mom or dad? We usually remember these words. They are powerful to us. We also can often remember hurtful words. They are also powerful. They are hard to forget sometimes.

The Bible reminds us to think about what we say. God reminds us to say things that help people and make them stronger. Not things that are harmful. What are some good words to say to others? Maybe, "Seeing you makes me feel happy." Or, "I think you're doing a good job." "How can I help?" "I like being with you." "You are not alone."

These types of words help people feel stronger. They are powerful in a good way. When we use words like this, we are doing good works! And we were made to do good works!

• • • • • •

BEDTIME PRAYER

Dear God, Help me use my words to help others become stronger tomorrow. Help me share the things you are teaching me.

59. Do What is Right

"Do what is right and fair. Be kind and merciful to each other." Zechariah 7:9

Do you know about Zacchaeus? He climbed a tree. He wanted to see Jesus. Do you know that Jesus went to his house? They had dinner there. Did you know about what he said when he talked with Jesus? He was very happy about Jesus and Jesus' way. He wanted to be like Jesus too. What did he say?

He said, "I will sell half of my stuff. And I will give that money to the poor." Wow. That's nice! Then he said, "If I took anybody's money, I will pay them back with extra!" He was a person who took money from people. He was a tax collector. And in his job, he took more money than he was asked to. That's not good, is it?

But, he met Jesus. Meeting Jesus changes a lot of people. Now Zacchaeus wanted to make the wrong things he did right. Do you ever want to do that? We can do that by saying, "Sorry," when we hurt someone. We can do it by telling others what we did that was wrong.

This is doing what is right and fair, like the verse says. This is doing good works!

● ● ● ● ● ●

BEDTIME PRAYER

Dear God, Please help me be right and fair. I want to be like Zacchaeus.

60. Addicted to Good Work

"The goodness you have makes you want to do good, and the faith you have makes you work. We pray that with his power God will help you do these things more and more. " 2 Thessalonians 1:11

What's something you love to do? Do you love drawing? Building? Listening to music? Is there something you are addicted to? Addicted means that it's really hard to stop doing. I used to be addicted to candy. I LOVED candy. I loved everything that was sweet. It was really hard for me not to eat something sweet. One of my girls is addicted to reading. She wants to read every day. She wants to read every time she's not busy.

God wants us to be addicted to good works. This Bible verse reminds us to ask God to help us. He can help us want to do good works more and more. We were made to do good works. And God will help us! Ask him to help you be addicted to good works!

BEDTIME PRAYER

Dear God, Please help me love to do good works for you! You are such a kind God. I want everyone to know how great you are!

PART SIX

Can God Use Me When I'm Young?

61. Jesus Loves Kids

"I tell you the truth. You must change and become like little children. If you don't do this, you will never enter the kingdom of heaven. The greatest person in the kingdom of heaven is the one who makes himself humble like this child." Matthew 18:2-4

Jesus really loves kids. He even tells the grown-ups to be like the kids! What does he mean? Why would he do that? Jesus told the grown-ups to be really great, you have to be like a child. The kind of "great" that Jesus is talking about is like "important." Maybe it means like, "If you want to be a star, you've got to be like a child."

Children have lots of great ideas, but they're not the boss. Right? Probably your mom or dad tell you to get ready for bed. They help get you to school. They may look at your homework. Moms, dads, and other adults help take care of kids. So, what does Jesus mean?

He means, "Kids have parents take care of them. Grownups need to know that God takes care of them too." Jesus tells the grownups to learn from kids! God wants to use you today!

● ● ● ● ● ●

BEDTIME PRAYER

Dear God, Thank you for using me now!

62. God Already Saved Me!

"The Lord saved me from a lion and a bear. He will also save me from this Philistine." 1 Samuel 17:37

David was the young son of Jesse. All his older brothers went to the army. But, David was made to stay home. He had to take care of the sheep. He was alone a lot. And he was young! Maybe just a little older than you. It always makes me happy to read about him. When he came to give food to his brothers, he saw Goliath. Goliath was really big. He kept yelling about how big he was. He kept saying how no one could kill him. All the men in the army stayed hidden.

David took one look at Goliath and said, "I'll go fight him!" At first, the king said no because David was only a boy. But David told him how he had to fight a lion and a bear. He said, "God already saved me from them. He will save me from Goliath too!"

God loves to use young people to do important things. God wants to use you today!

● ● ● ● ● ●

BEDTIME PRAYER

Dear God, Thanks for saving David from the lion and the bear. I want to trust you too. I want to help do your work.

63 Don't Hide!

"The angel of the Lord appeared to Gideon and said,
"The Lord is with you, mighty warrior!" Judges 6:12

Do you like to play hide-and-seek? I love it! I love to play in the dark too. Do you ever do that? We play in our house with all the lights off. It's so fun! It's a little scary, but not a bad scary. It's super fun to have a great hiding spot! I feel excited to listen to the person go right by me and not even know I'm there!

The angel of the Lord found Gideon when he was hiding! Gideon was young. He was taking the wheat grain off the stalk. And he was hiding while he did it. He was scared of the enemies that were nearby. But, God loves to use young people to do big jobs! He wanted Gideon to lead an army.

God told Gideon to do a special job. Gideon was scared. But if you read Judges 6, you can see that God helped him! Do you get scared too sometimes? God can help you too! He wants to help us not be afraid and trust him. What can you do tomorrow to share his love? He wants to use you!

● ● ● ● ● ●

BEDTIME PRAYER

Dear God, Thanks for helping me when I'm afraid. I want to do work for you while I'm young!

64. You Are an Example

"You are young, but do not let anyone treat you as if you were not important. Be an example to show the believers how they should live. Show them with your words, with the way you live, with your love, with your faith, and with your pure life." 1 Timothy 4:12

Sometimes big people don't listen to our ideas when we are young. Do you feel like that? Do you sometimes feel that you have a great idea, but nobody will listen? You've been reading about God every day. And, you know that Jesus loves kids. Jesus told big people to be like kids, right?

This verse tells us that we can know that we are important. We can show others the ways of Jesus. We can live with love. We can show others how to live with faith. This is a special job. God WANTS to use young kids to show his ways. You can show his ways at school. You can show his ways of love at home. He wants to use you right now!!

● ● ● ● ● ●

BEDTIME PRAYER

Dear God, Thank you for your special job. I want to show others your ways. You are loving and kind. I want to be loving and kind too!

65. You Can Help

"Continue to read the Scriptures to the people, strengthen them, and teach them. Do these things until I come. Remember to use the gift that you have." 1 Timothy 4:13-14

Paul was a great man of God. He told everyone about Jesus. He met Timothy. Timothy was young. But Paul saw Timothy loved God. Paul asked Timothy to help him. They told everyone about Jesus. Later, Paul was in jail. He wrote Timothy a letter. He told him to keep telling about Jesus. He said,"It's okay that you are young!" God loves to use young boys and girls!

This verse is from the letter Paul wrote. He told Timothy - keep reading the Bible! He said to teach everyone what he reads. He is young, but he can help!

God wants to use kids. You are young too, but you can help! You can show his love at home! You can show his love at school!

● ● ● ● ● ●

BEDTIME PRAYER

Dear God, Help me be like Timothy. I want to tell everyone about you!

66. Say What God Says

"You must go everywhere that I send you. You must say everything I tell you to say. Don't be afraid of anyone, because I am with you. I will protect you." Jeremiah 1:7-8

Have you ever felt scared to do something? I sure have! I did many plays in school. I was always scared. I sang solos sometimes. Always scared. I had to make new friends at a new school. Always scared! What do you do when you are scared? How do you help feel braver?

This verse is about a boy who felt like he was too young to help. You can read about him in chapter one of Jeremiah. God had a special job for him. He was scared, just like we have been.

Why does God tell him not to be afraid? Because he is with him. He told him that he would protect him and be with him. He even said he would tell him what to say. Wow! Do you think God can help you like that? 100% yes! He helped Jeremiah to tell others about him. He will help you too!

God loves to help children speak for him!

• • • • •

BEDTIME PRAYER

Dear God, Help me to never be afraid. I am glad that you are always with me!

67. The Right Place at the Right Time

"And who knows, you may have been chosen queen for just such a time as this." Esther 4:14

Esther was just a young teenager when she became queen. What would it be like to be 14 or 15 and be the queen? Wow. I can't imagine. The king made all the decisions. But the queen could sometimes talk to the king. And that is what Esther did. You can read her story in the Bible. The book is named after her! Esther.

There was a big plan to trick the king into killing God's people. But her uncle told her this verse, Esther 4:14. He said to her that she was not there by mistake. He said that God had put her there so that she could help her people.

And guess what?! It worked! The king listened to Queen Esther. He did not let Esther's people - God's people - die. Thanks, God, for making sure Esther was able to talk to the king!

Wherever you are is not a mistake either. Just like Esther, God made sure you were in your school and your neighborhood at this time. Why? What job does God have for you? God used Esther when she was young. God wants to use you too!

God loves to help children be brave!

• • • • • •

BEDTIME PRAYER

Dear God, what can I do tomorrow to help others?

68. Just a Lunch

"Here is a boy with five loaves of barley bread and two little fish. But that is not enough for so many people." ...Then Jesus took the loaves of bread. He thanked God for the bread and gave it to the people who were sitting there. He did the same with the fish." John 6:8, 11

Jesus did miracles all the time. He healed people. He stopped storms. He walked on water. He even gave people life after they died! He also fed BIG groups of people. Thousands of people. He did all of this with miracles.

Do you know how he fed 5,000 people in the book of Matthew, chapter 14? A little boy gave Jesus his lunch. This boy had a lunch sack that had five small loaves of bread and 2 fish. To many other big people, the little boy's lunch was nothing. But to Jesus, it was just what he wanted.

The little boy gave his lunch. Jesus thanked God for it. And then, it was given to EVERYONE for lunch! Amazing!

You never know what God will do! Would you give Jesus your lunch? Keep your eyes looking tomorrow. Maybe you can share something with someone!! It may feel so special to them!

- - - - - -

BEDTIME PRAYER

Dear God, Help me look for ways to share like that boy!

69. Special Jobs

*"And his sister stood far away to see what
would be done to him." Exodus 2:4*

Are you a big sister or a little sister? Do you have brothers or sisters? Are you an only child?   I am a big sister. I liked being the big sister. Sometimes I got to be the boss. Do you like to be the boss too?

This verse is about Miriam. She was the big sister to 2 brothers. One baby brother was named Moses. Do you know the story about him? Miriam watched baby Moses in the river. His mom hid him from bad men. And Miriam, who was maybe 7 years old, followed Moses' basket as it went down the river.

The princess went to the river. She found the basket with the baby. She kept the baby. This saved Moses' life! Miriam helped more. She told the princess that her mom can feed the baby. And the princess said okay!

Moses' mom fed the baby. Then he went to live with the princess. God used the baby's sister to help!

God loves to help children do special jobs!

● ● ● ● ● ●

BEDTIME PRAYER

Dear God, Thanks that little girls can do big jobs! That makes me feel happy. How can I help at home and at school?

70. I'm Talking to You!

Samuel said, "Speak, Lord. I am your servant, and I am listening." 1 Samuel 3:10b

My daughter woke me up one time. I was sleeping. I heard, "Mom... Mom...." I sat up. "Are you okay?" She was okay. She just needed help because she didn't feel well. Did you ever wake up in the middle of the night?

When Samuel was 11, he lived with the old man at the temple. The old man served God Day and night. Samuel had a special job to help the old man. He learned a lot about God there. One night he heard his name. "Samuel!" He thought it was the old man. But, when he came to see him, the man said it was not him. Samuel heard his name 3 times. "Samuel!" The old man understood that God was talking to Samuel. He told Samuel to stay in bed. He must listen to God's words. If God wants to talk to us, we listen!

God had a special message for the old man. He told it to Samuel. Samuel told it to the old man.

Did you know that God likes to talk to children?

Maybe he wants to say something special to you today!

● ● ● ● ● ●

BEDTIME PRAYER

Dear God, Help me hear from you too. I want to be like Samuel. Do you want me to tell someone about your love?

71. Hail the Young King

*"Josiah was eight years old when he became king.
He ruled 31 years in Jerusalem." 2 Chronicles 34:1*

Did you read that verse? An 8-year-old boy became king. Wow! His name was Josiah. He was very young. But, he was happy to learn about God. He is the king who helped get important parts of the Bible. He loved God from a young age. He helped God's people love God more and more.

Did you know that God loves for children to help? He loves for children to do important jobs. When children do special jobs for God, they surprise big people. Big people sometimes understand God more because of children.

It's important that you keep walking with God. Keep loving him. Keep reading the Bible. You never know what job God may have for you!

• • • • •

BEDTIME PRAYER

Dear God, thank you for asking children to help you! I want to help too. I want to help others love you more and more, too, like Josiah!

72. The Trusting Teenagers

"The God we serve is able to save us from the furnace and your power. If he does this, it is good. But even if God does not save us, we want you, our king, to know this: We will not serve your gods." Daniel 3:17, 18

You may know this Bible story. There were 3 men who wanted to only worship God. The king got very mad. He wanted them to worship a statue. These men said no. They said no even when the king said he would kill them! Wow! They are brave.

The king tried to kill them, but God saved them. It was a big miracle! The king wanted to worship God, too, then. These men were young. Some people who study the Bible think they were VERY young. They may have been young teenagers!

I don't know how old they were. But I would not be surprised if they were teenagers. God loves to use children to do big jobs! It was a big job to trust God. They did! And the king learned about God and his ways!

God can use you too!

$\bullet\ \bullet\ \bullet\ \bullet\ \bullet$

BEDTIME PRAYER

Dear God, thank you for saving those men. I know you are always with me. I can do important jobs for you!

PART SEVEN

But what if life is sad?

73. Strong Love

"Christ's love is greater than any person can ever know. But I pray that you will be able to know that love. Then you can be filled with the fullness of God." Ephesians 3:18, 19

Who is the strongest person you know? Did you ever see someone strong on TV? There are really strong people! I'm not very strong. I like to see strong people, though. One time I watched a man pull 12 cars with a big strap. 12! This verse reminds us that God's love is strong. Very strong. It's greater than a person can really understand. But Paul said that he would pray. He would pray for people to know how amazing God's love is. We can pray for that too!

Sometimes life can get sad. But God's love can be bigger than our sadness. It can be like the strongest person we know. God's love can help pull all our sadness away.

God cares about when you are sad!

• • • • • •

BEDTIME PRAYER

Dear God, I'm glad you care about me. I am glad your love is strong. Help me to remember that when I feel sad.

74. Sad Sin

"But if we confess our sins, he will forgive our sins. We can trust God. He does what is right. He will make us clean from all the wrongs we have done." 1 John 1:9

When I was little, my brother made me so mad. Sometimes I was so angry. I wanted to hurt him. I didn't. But he was so mean. I was mean, too, sometimes. One time I took his favorite toy. I hid it. I lied to him and said I didn't know where it was. I just was angry with him.

But that was wrong, wasn't it? I did feel bad. He looked everywhere for it. And then he cried. He cried a lot. I felt sad that I had done that. It didn't feel good to steal his toy and lie to him about it. I gave it back. He was really mad at me. And I felt icky.

This verse reminds us that God forgives our sins. We just tell him, and he forgives. He can clean all that icky out of our hearts. He forgives us! That's a very happy thing, isn't it?

God cares when you feel sad about your sin.

• • • • • •

BEDTIME PRAYER

Dear God, Thank you for forgiving me! Please help me to remember to ask you for forgiveness. Then I can feel happy about all the help you give!

75. It Doesn't Stay Forever

"...Crying may last for a night. But joy comes in the morning". Psalm 30:5

I had a cat. I named it Sissy La. Later I found out it was a boy. But his name was still Sissy La. It was a good, funny name. He was black. He had green eyes. He was very pretty! He didn't come inside. He ran all around. Sometimes he was gone for a few days. I didn't worry. I always knew my Sissy La would come back.

But, one day, he didn't. I called and called for him. We walked up and down the alley. No, Sissy La. The next day we saw him on the road. He had been hit. I didn't stop crying for a long time. I loved Sissy La so much.

Did you ever have a special pet? Do you feel sad when you think about it? Maybe a friend moved away. That can make us feel sad too. If we have a fight, we feel sad. Sometimes it's hard to stop crying; we feel so sad!

But this verse gives us hope. It says that sadness doesn't stay forever. It says happy feelings can come back. And, it's especially true when we know about God's love. His love gives us hope.

He cares when you feel sad!

• • • • •

BEDTIME PRAYER

Dear God, Thank you that sadness doesn't last forever.

76. Counting Tears

"You have recorded my troubles. You have kept a list of my tears. Aren't they in your records? " Psalm 56:8

What do you do when you feel sad? What helps you feel better? My oldest girl likes to listen to music. She cries and listens to music. My youngest daughter likes to old her bear. She has a bear from when she was little. She loves to hold it and cry. If I need to cry, I go to my bed. I like my bed, and it helps me to be there.

Where do you go? What do you do?

I like this verse. It tells us that God sees our sad times. He sees what is hard and sad for us. He even knows every time we cry. It makes me feel a little happier to know that. I like to know that God sees and understands. He doesn't say, "Don't cry!" He says, "I understand."

God cares about when you feel sad! He is seeing every tear. You are not alone in your sadness.

● ● ● ● ● ●

BEDTIME PRAYER

Dear God, I'm glad I'm not alone. Thank you for always being with me. I feel better when I know you are close.

77. Hope in God

*"Why am I so sad? Why am I so upset? I should put
my hope in God. I should keep praising him,
my Savior and my God." Psalm 42:11*

Do you know about Jonah? Yes, he's the one who rode in a big fish. God sent one to take him to the beach. You know, most people know Jonah because of that ride in the fish. That's a miracle! But I think we should remember Jonah's attitude. He had a bad one! He was angry and sad at God. He was really not happy. Do you know why? He told a big city about God. And the people listened. They wanted to know God. That made him mad! Why?

Who knows! Sometimes we all have bad attitudes. We can feel sad about something little. We can feel mad about something that we really shouldn't. We all can be like Jonah. So we need to remember this verse.

We can tell ourselves about things that are true. I can put my hope in God. I can keep praising him.

God cares about how we feel! Let's be careful to make sure that we don't have bad attitudes like Jonah, though!!

• • • • • •

BEDTIME PRAYER

Dear God, Help me remember to have a good attitude. I am glad you care about how I feel. I want to put my hope in you!

78. A Broken Heart

"The Lord is close to the brokenhearted. He saves those whose spirits have been crushed." Psalm 34:18

Joseph is a bold kid. He has some dreams. His brothers are all bowing to him in the dreams. Joseph is young. He doesn't think about it. He just goes ahead and tells his older brothers about his dreams. Would you tell your brother? If I told my brother that, he would be mad! He would say, "No way!"

That's how Joseph's brothers felt too. They did not want to bow down to Joseph. Joseph was already his dad's favorite son. That didn't help. So all the brothers were mad. They sold him into slavery. How do you think that would feel?

I think Joseph had a broken heart. This verse is good for people who feel their heart was broken. Joseph felt it. I've felt it. Maybe you have felt it too. This verse is so wonderful. It reminds us of a promise. A promise that God is close to us. He comes close in a special way when our heart is broken.

He cares when your heart is broken. He comes close to help you.

• • • • •

BEDTIME PRAYER

Dear God, Thank you that you come close to me. Thank you that you can help my broken heart.

79. See His Love

"The Lord shows his true love every day. At night I have a song, and I pray to my living God." Psalm 42:8

Can you think of a way that God shows his love? How does he show his love every day? Can you think of ways he cares for you? Can you think of ways he loves you?

We talked about how God made everything. We talked about how he plans everything. We talked about how God planned you. How does he take care of you and the earth you live on?

Today I had food. The sun was shining. It was cloudy, but still, the sun was there. I saw beautiful flowers. I played with my dog. I read the Bible. I wrote to you. My day was not perfect. But I can see God's love. His love doesn't make perfect days. His love loves us even on hard days.

Some days are sad days. Some days are mad days. You can always practice looking for his love. Seeing his love will help you feel better.

He cares about how you feel and shows you his love.

BEDTIME PRAYER

Dear God, Thank you for your promises. Help me see your love even when I feel sad.

80. Run to Jesus

"If you come back to me and trust me, you will be saved. If you will be calm and trust me, you will be strong." Isaiah 30:15

Sometimes how we feel can take over. We can't think. Maybe we don't pray. Sometimes I eat more sugar when I feel sad. I feel bad after I eat it. Sometimes I can hide a little bit. I go to my room. Maybe I just stay there for a long time.

This verse tells us how to get away from those feelings. We can feel sad sometimes. But maybe it's too sad. And sadness takes over. Maybe your friend said something mean. Maybe you said something mean. Maybe you lost something important. Maybe you lost something that wasn't yours.

There is a way to get away from those feelings. We run to Jesus. When we run to God, we can feel calmer. We can practice trusting him.

God cares about how you feel. He wants to help you!

● ● ● ● ● ●

BEDTIME PRAYER

Dear God, Thank you for all the promises to help me! I am happy that you talk so much about helping. I feel stronger when I read about you! I love you!

81. Sharing in Sadness

"The Lord hears good people when they cry out to him. He saves them from all their troubles." Psalm 34:17

In 1 Kings 17, there is an amazing story. There is a woman with a sick son. Her husband died. That's sad, right? Well, there is also no food in the land. Everyone is hungry. She and her son are very hungry. She is getting sticks to make a fire. She has enough stuff to make one more loaf of bread. She will make the last small piece of bread. How sad do you think she feels?

There is a man of God who comes. He asks her from a glass of water. She is sad. She is working. But she helps him anyways. She brings him water. He also asks her for bread. O my! She has so little. What will she tell him?

She makes the bread and shares it with him. Wow! She is sad and needs bread too. God blesses the woman so that she always has flour and oil to make bread. Every time she looked in the jar - there was flour and oil. Also, God healed her sick son!

God will help us to help others even when we feel sad.

BEDTIME PRAYER

Dear God, Help me remember how you helped this woman. I want to trust you just like she did.

82. He Knows

*"Lord, you know everything I want. My cries
are not hidden from you." Psalm 38:9*

Do you ever wish your friend knew what you were thinking? Maybe she has a delicious cookie. You look at it and think, "Boy, I'd like her to share it with you." But she doesn't. She just eats all of her cookies and licks her fingers! Then maybe you feel mad or sad. She might look at your face and say, "What?" If you tell her you wanted a bite, what could she say back?

I would say, "Well, I didn't know! Why didn't you say something?" We have to talk about our feelings. We have to share our thoughts, so others know, right?

I hope this verse is a good one for you. It reminds us that God knows everything. He hears our cries. He hears our prayers. All our heart is before him. It's good to tell God your feelings and your thoughts. That's being a friend with God. He listens to us. And we listen to him. That's being good friends.

God is a good friend when you feel sad.

● ● ● ● ● ●

BEDTIME PRAYER

Dear God, Thank you for being my friend. Help me to remember to tell you all my feelings.

83. Hope and Joy and Peace

"I pray that the God who gives hope will fill you with much joy and peace while you trust in him. Then your hope will overflow by the power of the Holy Spirit." Romans 15:13

Do you feel mostly happy or mostly sad? Some people are happy a lot. It's just the way God made them. But not everyone is like that. Some people feel sad sometimes. Some people can feel sad a lot. It's different for everyone. I feel mostly happy. But my sister feels sad more. It's okay to feel sad.

But, I want you to know that I am praying this verse for you. Paul wrote this verse in the Bible. He prayed for the people to feel hope. But not just hope. Also, he prayed for hope and joy, and peace! That's a lot of good feelings. I am praying for you right now as I write. I want you to have hope and joy and peace too! I want your hope to be stronger than your sadness.

God cares about when you are sad. He wants to give you hope and joy and peace!

BEDTIME PRAYER

Dear God, Thank you that we can pray and ask you for help. I want to feel hope and joy, and peace. Can you help me, please?

84. No More Tears

*"He will wipe away every tear from their eyes.
There will be no more death, sadness, crying, or pain.
All the old ways are gone." Revelation 21:4*

Did you ever cry so much and so hard that you ran out of tears? They were just gone. And you were just done crying. I did before. When I was little, sometimes I cried that hard.

This verse is so neat! This is a great promise. Just think. One day there will be no more sadness. When we are with him forever, he will wipe every tear from our eyes. We won't run out. He will take them out! There won't be crying or pain. Isn't that exciting? I feel so happy that God understands our sadness. And I feel so happy that when we are in heaven with Him, there won't be any sadness!

He gives us a promise for when we feel sad. The promise is: it won't always be like this!

He cares when you feel sad!

• • • • • •

BEDTIME PRAYER

Dear God, Thank you for this promise. Thank you that some-day I won't feel sad ever again. That's amazing! Thank you for helping me.

PART EIGHT

But what if life is hard?

85. As Sure as the Sun

"I will make you strong and will help you. I will help you with my right hand that saves you." Isaiah 41:10

Life can get hard. Homework is hard. Our friend says something mean. Maybe we have to move. Maybe our parents have to work a lot. Or a pet dies. Or our teacher doesn't help us. Or it rains when we need it sunny. The Bible has a lot to say about hard lives.

Life is hard sometimes. It just is. Jesus even said that in John 16, "In this world you will have trouble." It's as sure as the sun coming up in the morning. But, do you know what Jesus said right after that? He said, "But be brave! I have defeated the world!"

Verses like these in John and Isaiah tell us a good truth. Hard times don't stay forever. We can be brave because we know Jesus. We can ask him for help! He says that he will help us.

Remember in hard times who Jesus is. Trust in him.

• • • • •

BEDTIME PRAYER

Dear God, Can you help me to know who you are? Please remind me to ask you for help. Thank you for your love!

86. Jesus is so kind

"The Lord gives strength to those who are tired. He gives more power to those who are weak." Isaiah 40:29

Jesus is so kind. I love that about him. He looks for those who are having a hard time. And then, he helps them. He looks for those who feel that their sin is so big. Then he shows them forgiveness.

In John 5, it tells about the man who had a hard time moving. It doesn't say what his illness was. It doesn't say why he had a hard time moving. It doesn't say if anyone helped him get there. It doesn't say if he had a family. But we can know that life was hard for him.

The Bible says that Jesus saw him and asked him, "Do you want to be healed?" Jesus **saw** him. This man didn't know who Jesus was. Jesus was looking around and saw this man who had been sick for 38 years.

Jesus cares about your life. God is looking to help his children.

Remember in hard times who Jesus is. Trust in him.

BEDTIME PRAYER

Dear God, Thank you for the kindness of Jesus. Thank you that you see the hard times in my life. I want to trust you.

87. Relax

"So don't worry about tomorrow. Today has enough worries of its own. Tomorrow will have its own worries." Mathew 6:34

One of my girls' worries. She worries about a lot of things. She worries about her sister. She worries about the dog. She worries about her homework. She worries about new friends. She worries about her life when she is grown up. Do you ever worry? How was your day today? Was there something hard today?

This verse tells us what Jesus said. What did he say? Can you read it again?

He said NOT to worry, right? He said to think about today. And then tomorrow, we can think about tomorrow.

Jesus doesn't mean that we can't make plans. Jesus means we can relax about tomorrow. If there are hard times today, let's think about those. Jesus will help us today. And you know what? He will help us tomorrow too. I tell my daughter this too! Let's just think about today.

Remember in hard times who Jesus is. Trust in him.

• • • • • •

BEDTIME PRAYER

Dear God, Sometimes I worry when things get hard. Can you help me trust you? Help me to think about today. And ask you for help today. Then, we can do it tomorrow together.

88. You can Say It

"People, trust God all the time. Tell him all your problems. God is our protection. "Psalm 62:8

Did you know it's good for us to talk? Ha! Sometimes I ask my girls to stop talking. But, it's really good for us. It is really good for us to say out loud important feelings. Sometimes we feel sad, or mad, or hurt. It is good for our hearts and our minds to tell someone. Is it hard for you to talk about how you feel?

It used to be hard for me. But now I see how it helps to get things off of my mind. I feel better.

God knows he made us this way. He knows that it is healthy to talk about our problems. Look at this verse. It tells us to do just that! We can tell him - out loud - our problems. It helps us to feel better. It helps us to know that God is our friend.

Remember in hard times who Jesus is. Trust in him. Talk to him.

• • • • • •

BEDTIME PRAYER

Dear God, Please help me to talk to you. Sometimes I forget. But I can see you want me to know you are my friend. You want me to know that I can tell you all my problems. Thank you for that!

89. Bad Things Made Better

"We know that in everything God works for the good of those who love him." Romans 8:28

Some days I can't do anything right. I drop stuff. I break stuff. I say stuff. I forget to do what I said I would do. I can't find my phone. The dog puts a hole in my favorite shirt. I can't find my favorite shorts. It can sometimes feel that ALL day it's just not my day.

That's when I love this verse the most. It tells me that even the "bad" stuff, the not-so-fun stuff is okay. It's okay because somehow, God can work it for my good.

Do you remember that story about Joseph? His brothers sold him to be a slave because they were so mad. That was not a good day for Joseph. But God worked things for good. Do you know that story? Later, Joseph helped the king! He got to be a boss that helped the king. And God used Joseph to help save many lives during a famine.

Remember in hard times that God will work this for good.

● ● ● ● ● ●

BEDTIME PRAYER

Dear God, Please help me remember Joseph. Help me to remember how you work good things from bad things. I want to trust you.

90. What Does God Think?

*"The Lord your God is with you. The mighty One will save you.
The Lord will be happy with you. You will rest in his love.
He will sing and be joyful about you." Zephaniah 3:17*

Do you ever feel like everyone is mad at you at the same time?
We can feel this way sometimes. It feels really sad and hard.
But I love this verse! This verse makes me feel happy! "The
Lord will be happy with you." That makes me feel hope.

Do you know about Noah? Everyone was not happy with
him. Many people thought he was crazy. But Noah did what
God asked him to do. He knew that he wanted the Lord to be
happy with him. He wanted that more than he wanted other
people to be happy with him. Do you know what he did? He
built a big boat before God sent the flood.

Remember in hard times that God will help you! And remember that what he thinks is more important than anybody else!

● ● ● ● ● ●

BEDTIME PRAYER

Dear God, Thank you for Noah's life. Thank you that he listened to you. I want to listen to you too! Thank you that you
are happy that I am your child! I am happy too!

91. God Makes a Team

*"Give your worries to the Lord.
He will take care of you." Psalm 55:22*

God told Moses to speak to the king. He told him that he would tell him what to say. But Moses was worried about something. Do you know what it was? He was worried about talking to the king. He had a hard time speaking! Sometimes his words came out wrong. Sometimes he repeated himself. He thought the king didn't want to listen to him.

So Moses told God how he felt. He told him his problems. And God said that Moses could take his brother with him. God handled Moses' hard time for him. He did it by giving him a friend. God told Moses the plan. God would tell Moses what to say. Moses would tell his brother what God said. And his brother would tell the king. Great idea, God!

If you read the story in Exodus 7 and 8, you can see that sometimes even Moses did speak! God gave Moses a team to do the job!

Remember to ask God for help! He is always your friend. Sometimes he may send more friends too!!

● ● ● ● ● ●

BEDTIME PRAYER.

Dear God, Thank you for caring about how I feel. Thank you for helping Moses. Thank you for helping me!!

92. What are You Carrying?

*"Come to me, all of you who are tired and have heavy loads.
I will give you rest." Mathew 11:28*

One summer, my family went camping. We had tents. We had sleeping bags. We had food. But this trip was different. We were not staying at a campsite. We were hiking. We were hiking back into the woods to camp. We had to carry everything. Everything we could need or want. We wanted to camp there for 3 days. We had a lot of stuff to carry!

Think about your life. What kinds of things do you have to carry? I don't mean sleeping bags. I don't mean your bag for school. I mean things like - sadness, anger, frustration. We can feel these feelings when things don't happen the way we want them to. Or if they don't happen the way they "should." It can happen when we make bad choices. It's a lot for us to carry around.

That's why Jesus said this verse. He wants to carry those feelings for you. He wants to forgive you and help you!

Give him all your problems!

BEDTIME PRAYER

Dear God, Thank you that you want to help me! I need your help! Thank you for carrying my feelings for me!

93. God Knows

"But not even one of the little birds can die without your Father's knowing it. God even knows how many hairs are on your head. So don't be afraid. You are worth much more than many birds." Matthew 10:29-31

I like to go to nature centers. Many have a room with big windows. There are benches there. I can sit and watch the many birds who come and eat at the feeders. It's very relaxing for me. I can listen to them talk and sing. I can watch them fly around and back and forth. One time a hawk came and sat in the tree. I thought maybe he would eat a bird!

He didn't eat one while I was there. But I thought of this verse when I saw that hawk. I don't know what happened after I left. But God does! He knows everything! He knows every time a bird dies!

I like this verse because, in the end, it says, "You are worth much more than many birds." He keeps track of all the birds in all the world. He cares even more for you, though. Don't let your hard times overwhelm you. God is always with you!

· · · · · ·

BEDTIME PRAYER

Dear God, I am so glad that you know everything. It makes me feel happy and safe that you are always here for me.

94. Find Your Strength

"David found strength in the Lord his God." 1 Samuel 30:6

I had to move. Again. My family moved a few times when I was growing up. The big problem was leaving my best friend. Her name was Sarah. She lived right down the street. We rode bikes together. We played at the park together. She was very important to me. My heart felt broken.

David was leading an army. They came back to a city where their families were. They found out the enemy had come. All their families were taken as prisoners. David was so sad. His heart was broken.

But the Bible says he found strength in the Lord. Some Bibles say that David encouraged himself in the Lord.   David reminded himself about God. He reminded himself about the truths of God. This helped David to get up and get busy! He asked the Lord what to do. And the Lord told him to chase the enemy down and save the families!

Remember to think about God's truths when you are in a hard time! It will help you. Then, ask God what to do next!

• • • • • •

BEDTIME PRAYER

Dear God, Can you help me to remember who you are? Can you help me to learn truths about you? I want to find my strength in you as David did!

95. Ask Him

"People in trouble look to you for help, God.
You are the one who helps the orphans." Psalm 10:14

If your pet was sick, who can you call for help? The vet, right? If you don't understand the homework, who can help? Maybe your teacher or a parent. If you get hurt at school, can you go to the nurse? We know how to get help from lots of people. This is good! This verse reminds us that it is good to ask God for help too!

People who know God will look to God for help. We have to remind ourselves sometimes. We have lots of people to help us. So sometimes we can forget to ask him too. We should ask people for help. God has given people into our lives to help us. But, also we can ask him. This is part of having a friendship with him. We can tell him when life is hard. We do both: ask God and ask people.

Remember that God cares about how you feel. He will help you! He will give you people to help you too!

● ● ● ● ● ●

BEDTIME PRAYER

Dear God, Thanks for helping me! I'm really glad you give doctors, teachers, parents, and ______________. Help me remember to ask you for help too!

96. It's Worth It

"Trust the Lord with all your heart. Don't depend on your own understanding." Proverbs 3:5

My daughter did not want to go to the state track meet. It felt like too much pressure. She did not want to race. She just liked to run. She came to me crying. She asked me not to make her go. I felt really sad, but I told her she had to go. Her team needed her. She had to finish the season. Plus, she needed this chance. This chance could help her be strong in her mind. Her legs were strong. She was fast. But her mind didn't want to do it. She needed a little stronger mind.

Do you know what happened? She was super nervous, but she did it! She went to state and was glad she did! She had a great time! Sometimes we have to do what a parent or a teacher says. Maybe we don't agree, but we have to.

Same with God. Sometimes life seems difficult. We think we should do it a different way.

But remember to trust God. He will help you through it. And you will know him better and trust him more after it.

* * * * *

BEDTIME PRAYER

Dear God, Please help me remember to trust you. I know you care about me!

PART NINE

But what if I'm scared?

97. New Leader Fears

*"The Lord himself will go before you. He will be with you.
He will not leave you or forget you. Don't be afraid.
Don't worry." Deuteronomy 31:8*

I love this part of the Bible. Moses has been a strong leader. He has helped people know God and follow His ways. But, He knows He will not be the leader anymore. It's time for Joshua to be the leader. And Joshua is getting ready to lead God's people into a battle.

First, Moses tells the people not to be afraid because God is with them. Then, Moses tells Joshua not to be afraid because God is with him. God knows that people will be nervous about Moses not being the leader. God knows that Joshua will be scared to be the new leader.

Do you get scared sometimes when you have to do something new or by yourself? It's normal for us to feel scared. But, who do we run to, Girls? We run to God! He is with us.

God cares about when you feel scared! He wants you to ask him for help. He loves you!

• • • • •

BEDTIME PRAYER

Dear God, Thank you for speaking through Moses. Thank you for speaking to me! Help me remember to trust you with all my fears.

98. Worrying Warthog

"I leave you peace. My peace I give you. I do not give it to you as the world does. So don't let your hearts be troubled. Don't be afraid." John 14:27

Did you ever see a warthog? If you get a chance to look it up, do it! They are funny-looking. I think they're kind of ugly. They have weird, wiry hair. They have big growths or "warts" on their faces. They have tusks coming out the sides of their mouths. They have baggy eyes. I'm not joking. They look weird. But when they are little, they are kind of cute. They still have weird, wiry hair. But everything is just small and cute on them.

This verse says to not let our hearts be troubled. Troubled means worry. And worry is like the baby of Fear. Sometimes it's small and doesn't seem like a big deal. But it can grow into an ugly adult called Fear. It's like a warthog! Both fear and worry will keep us from doing what God has called us to do.

God cares about when you feel worried or afraid. Always remember that he does not want your hearts troubled.

● ● ● ● ●

BEDTIME PRAYER

Dear God, It's hard to not worry. But I know you want what is best for me. Please help me trust you and not let my worries grow!

99. Need a Band-Aid?

"Do not worry about anything. But pray and ask God for everything you need. And when you pray, always give thanks. And God's peace will keep your hearts and minds in Christ Jesus. The peace that God gives is so great that we cannot understand it." Philippians 4:6-7

When you get a little scrape or cut, what do you do? Does your mom help you clean it? Do you do it by yourself? When it's all clean, what do you put on it?

I cleaned out my girl's little scratch. She was running in the woods. A branch scraped her leg. We washed it out, and then we put a band-aid on it.

Praying is like washing out your scrape. And giving thanks is like the band-aid. These verses tell us when we pray to God and give thanks to God, we are going to the right place for help. God says when we do this, his peace will be in our hearts and minds. And that we can't really understand how amazing his peace is, but we can have it.

Make sure you wash your worries and fears with prayer. Then, put on your thankful band-aid!

* * *

BEDTIME PRAYER

Dear God, Thank you that you are with me when I am worried and afraid. Help me to remember to pray to you and ask for help!

100. Get Rid of Fear

"When I am afraid, I will trust you. I praise God for his word. I trust God. So I am not afraid." Psalm 56:3-4

Maybe you know that David was a king in the Bible. But do you know about him before that? We have talked about how he fought the giant. Do you remember that? After he fought the giant, he was a helper to the king. But the king was mad when he understood that God wanted David to be the next king. And David had to run away to save his life.

There were good times and bad times while David was hiding. But he wrote these verses during a hard time. He had many enemies. But read again what David wrote. "When I am afraid, I will trust you." Sometimes we feel afraid. David says he will trust God when he feels afraid. Then he says, "I trust God. So I am not afraid."

Trust in God can help get rid of fear. When we are afraid, we trust him. And when we trust him, we are not afraid. Thanks, God!

• • • • • •

BEDTIME PRAYER

Dear God, Help me to be like David, please and trust you when I feel afraid.

101. Times of Trouble

"God is our protection and our strength.
He always helps in times of trouble." Psalm 46:1

There are lots of examples in the Bible of people being afraid. We can read about how they were afraid and how God helped them. The message to us over and over is to not be afraid but to trust God.

This verse reminds us that God is our protection. We have lots of helpers around us. God has given us lots of help. Maybe you have: teachers, parents, grandparents, neighbors, church leaders, and policemen to help keep you safe. All in all, they are from God. It is God who protects us. It is God who gives us strength. It is God who helps in times of trouble.

It is good for us to remind ourselves of this. Wherever we go, we can remember that God is with us. "He always helps in times of trouble." It's like when we are afraid, we can hide in God. We can run to Him in prayer.

God is a good hiding place for you! God is a good help for you!

- - - - -

BEDTIME PRAYER

Dear God, Thank you for always helping. Thank you for caring about me. Please always help me remember who you are! I want to trust you more.

102. Courage

"God did not give us a spirit that makes us afraid. He gave us a spirit of power and love and self-control. "2 Timothy 1:7

How do you feel when you spend the night at a new friend's? Or when you try out for a new sports team? What if you have to speak in front of a group? Do you feel afraid to tell some-one about Jesus? Or to make a new friend? Or, swim in a lake? I feel a little afraid to swim in a lake! Some things in life feel a little scary, right?

This verse reminds us that God does not give us fear. He gives us power or courage. That means that he helps us be brave. He helps us push our fears away. We can try new things!

What's something new that you've been afraid to try? Can you pray about it? You can ask for God's help. What can God help you do tomorrow?

• • • • • •

BEDTIME PRAYER

Dear God, Thank you that you give me courage. Help me to come to you for help to push away my fears. Show me what I can do tomorrow for you and help me not be afraid to do it!

103. Being Blind

*"Give all your worries to him, because
he cares for you."* 1 Peter 5:7

Have you ever seen a blind person before?   I have a friend who is blind. She has a dog who helps her. She also has some good friends who help her too. Imagine you are blind. What kind of things would you be worried about? What would make you feel scared?

We understand a lot of things by using our eyes. There is a lot you don't know when you are blind. You don't know that the sidewalk ends soon. You don't know how deep the pool is. You don't know how many books are on the shelf. There are a lot of unknowns.

We can see fine with our eyes and still be worried about unknowns. We can worry about a big test coming up. We can worry about our friends. We can worry about our parents and grandparents. This verse tells us to give all those worries to God. We can tell him all the things that we are worried about - known and unknown.

He cares for you!

● ● ● ● ● ●

BEDTIME PRAYER

Dear God, Thank you for caring about me! Thank you that I can give you all my worries. Please help me with __________. I am worried about it, but I want to trust you instead.

104. Remember Jesus

Then those who were in the boat worshiped Jesus and said, "Truly you are the Son of God!" Matthew 14:33

Do you remember this story? Jesus feeds A LOT of people. And he did with one boy's lunch. Amazing! Then he tells his friends to take the boat across the lake. He did not go in the boat. He went to pray. Later the weather was very windy. The waves got really big. It was hard for the boat to cross the lake. But, in the middle of the night, Jesus came to them. He came by walking on water! That was surprising!!

The Bible says the men were so scared. They did not think it could be Jesus. Jesus told Peter he could come out on the water too. Peter did! He walked on water with Jesus. But he stopped looking at Jesus. He was starting to look at the waves. Peter started to feel scared. Jesus helped him back to the boat. The wind stopped when Jesus and Peter were back in the boat.

The men said, "Truly, you are the Son of God!" Remind your-self who Jesus is to fight your fears too!

BEDTIME PRAYER

Dear God, You are great and powerful! Help me remember that. I won't feel afraid when I remember who you are!

105. Are There Sharks?

"I asked the Lord for help, and he answered me.
He saved me from all that I feared." Psalm 34:4

Do you like to play in the water? Would you jump into a pool? Would you jump into a lake? Would you jump into the ocean? Which one of those sounds the scariest? I don't like jumping into the water when I can't see the bottom. I feel afraid about not being able to see if the bottom is mucky. Or if there are fish right there. Or if there are sharks there.

There are lots of things that can make us feel afraid at times. Psalm 34:4 is a good reminder for us! We can ask the Lord for help. Actually, when David wrote this psalm, he was in a scary situation himself. He was hiding from two different kings! But this is the prayer he prayed, "Lord, please help!"

We've talked several times about asking the Lord for help. It's the best thing to do, isn't it?

Ask the Lord for help. He will answer you.

BEDTIME PRAYER

Dear God, Thank you for helping David. Thank you for helping me to remember that you will help me too. Please save me from all that, I fear.

106. The Best Hiding Spot

"You are my hiding place. You protect me from my troubles. You fill me with songs of salvation." Psalm 32:7

Do you play hide and seek? Where is the best place to hide in your house? When I was young, we had a great basement for hiding. There were several rooms down there. There were lots of things to hide behind. I LOVED hiding from my brother in the smallest storage room there. He had a hard time finding me.

This verse reminds us who is our help when things get hard. He can be our hiding place. You can hide all your heart with all of your worries and fears in him, just like I hid in that storage room. We do this when we go to Him with all our feelings. We have been talking about running to him, praying to him, asking him for help. These are ways that we can "hide." We give all these things to him. Then, we can try singing a song to him. We can remind ourselves of true things about God.

He cares about how you feel! He wants to help you.

● ● ● ● ● ●

BEDTIME PRAYER

Dear God, Thank you for being a hiding place for me. Help me to trust you with all my feelings.

107. Jesus Gives Peace

*"I leave you peace. My peace I give you. I do not give it t
o you as the world does. So don't let your hearts be
troubled. Don't be afraid." John 14:27*

In this verse, Jesus tells his friends he is leaving soon. How do you think they feel about that? Do you think they feel sad? I would feel sad. Jesus is amazing! But it's almost time for him to go back to heaven. One thing he promises to leave is peace. Peace is an important feeling. It's a feeling of calm. It's a feeling of safety and trust.

Then Jesus says something weird. "I do not give it to you as the world does." What does he mean? How do people get peace if they don't know Jesus? People feel calm and safe when things are good. If they get a good grade on their test, it feels good. If they get what they want for their birthday, that's great. When people are nice, it feels calm inside.

But Jesus gives us peace by telling us true things about himself. If you read John 14, you can see that Jesus is taking care of everything. So, you can have peace!

BEDTIME PRAYER

Dear God, Please help me remember to come to you for peace. I want to trust you more and more!

108. You are Not Alone

"We know that in everything God works for the good of those who love him. They are the people God called because that was his plan." Romans 8:28

Jesus had hard and scary things in his life too. What was the hardest, do you think? I think the hardest was going to die. Do you remember when Jesus is praying? He is in the garden. He asks Father God if there is a different way. Jesus says that if he has to die, he will. But, it's a very troubling time, isn't it?

Here are some things that are true about hard, scary times, friends. We will have them.   Sometimes God saves us from hard times. If not, then he goes with us through hard times. And he ALWAYS brings good from them.

We have talked about many stories from the Bible. You can remember the ways God helped others when they were scared and when life was hard. Help yourself remember true things about God. Try to memorize important verses to help you think about God's truths.

You are not alone. God is with you. If you think about truths, you have less time to think about your fears.

BEDTIME PRAYER

Dear God, Help me to remember true things about you. You are amazing. When I remember that, I feel safe.

PART TEN

Some Things to Remember

109. Never-Ending God

"Honor and glory to the King that rules forever! He cannot be destroyed and cannot be seen. Honor and glory forever and ever to the only God. Amen." 1 Timothy 1:17

It rained one July. I mean, it rained A LOT. We got so much rain that our basement flooded. I cleaned out all the things that were ruined. I found a wet, soggy brown box. In this box were all our Christmas ornaments. I used to buy a new ornament every year for my girls. I looked at each one. They were dirty. The colors were ruined. It was sad. I cried a little bit. I looked at each one trying to make my mind take a picture of it. I wanted to remember each one and why I bought it.

Do you know many times in the Bible, it talks about how God lives forever? He never had a start. He just was always there. And he will never have an end. He will always be. Doesn't that feel good? God is always here. He knows all of history and all of the future. That makes me feel stronger to just know him!

• • • • • •

BEDTIME PRAYER

Dear God, You are the king that rules forever. I am so glad that you cannot be destroyed. I praise your name!

110. Your Name

"From the ground, God formed every wild animal and every bird in the sky. He brought them to the man so the man could name them. Whatever the man called each living thing, that became its name." Genesis 2:19

Do you know how many bones are in your neck? Seven. Yep, only seven. Okay, now guess, how many bones are in a giraffe's neck? SEVEN! Can you believe it? I was so surprised when I read that! The giraffe's neck is longer than my whole body! There are only seven bones working together to hold that long neck up. Wow, God!

God made many beautiful and special animals. Then, he gave Adam the job of giving each animal a name. Adam had a very big job! What would you have named a giraffe? The old word for giraffe means "fast walker." Names are really important to God. They are important to us too. Your name is important because it means YOU. When mom says your name, you know who she's talking to. And now, when someone says giraffe, you will know it's that really tall animal with only seven bones in its neck!

• • • • •

BEDTIME PRAYER

Dear God, You are really amazing. You create many wonderful things. And that means me too. Thank you for making me and for knowing my name!!

111. You Can't Hide from God

"No one can hide where I cannot see him,' says the Lord.
'I fill all of heaven and earth,' says the Lord." Jeremiah 23:24

Did you ever hide from someone? I love to play hide and seek! When I was in 4th grade, I used to climb trees with my best friend in our neighborhood. We would bring food with us sometimes and have a "picnic" in the tree. It was fun! I especially loved it when someone walked by. My friend and I would be very quiet. The people wouldn't even know we were there. We could see them, but they didn't see us. We felt like we were spying on them. And, we kind of were, weren't we?

We can't hide from God, though. He sees everything, everywhere, all the time. The Bible says that he fills up the earth. There is nowhere you can go that he is not there. I like to think about this. It makes me feel good that he sees me and knows what is happening in my life. It's amazing that he can see you and me at the same time!

BEDTIME PRAYER

Dear God, It's awesome that you can see everywhere at the same time! I can't imagine being able to do that. You are a very amazing God.

112. Always Watching

"The Lord's eyes see everything that happens." Proverbs 15:3

Did you ever hear that phrase about "having eyes in the back of your head"? It means that the person wasn't looking but still knows what happened. Sometimes I felt like my mom had eyes in the back of her head. When I was little, my mom often knew what I had done even when she wasn't with me. One time she was outside working in the garden, and I ate a pudding. I wasn't allowed to. But I did it. She knew it was me and not my brother. How did she know that? I don't know, but she knew!

In a much bigger way, God knows everything too. He is never out back in the garden. He fills up everywhere on earth. There is nowhere that we can go that he is not there. He is with you right now in your room. And he is here with me in my room. He is in both places at the same time. He is at school, at home, at the store, at the park all at once. Isn't that amazing? He is such a powerful god!

● ● ● ● ●

BEDTIME PRAYER

Dear God, Thank you for always being here. Thank you for always watching, always knowing. Please help me make good decisions that show others your ways.

113. God's Friend

"And Abraham was called "God's friend." James 2:23

Do you know about Abraham? He was a man who loved God. He tried to trust God. Sometimes he did a good job. Sometimes he didn't. When he did a bad job, he said he was sorry. But do you know what the Bible says about Abraham? It says, "Abraham was called 'God's friend.'" That's a great thing! I want to be God's friend too.

Abraham trusted God. He always wanted to do what God said. Sometimes he made mistakes. But he told God he was sorry. Then he got right back to listening to God. Do you want to do that too? Do you want to trust him and listen to him?

Remember in easy times and hard times that God is your friend. I think talking out loud to him helps me. It helps me think about God being with me. It helps me remember that he is my friend. You can try it too. Just tell him how you feel. Ask him what to do. Friends can do that.

● ● ● ● ● ●

BEDTIME PRAYER

Dear God, Thank you for being my friend! Please help me remember that you are my friend. I never want to forget how much you love and care for me. I love you too!

114. God's Secrets

"Is there someone who worships the Lord? The Lord will point him to the best way. The Lord tells his secrets to those who respect him. He tells them about his agreement." Psalm 25:12,14

Jesus went to many places with his friends. He always told people about God's kingdom. He always helped people. He told people how to walk in God's ways. Some people loved to listen to him. Sometimes they made a big group and went with him. They all wanted to hear him. They all wanted to know him more.

Do you want to hear him too? Do you want to know him? I do! God still talks today. He uses the Bible to show us his ways. He uses the Bible to show us his heart. When we read it, we are hearing him!

Try to read the Bible every day so you can know Jesus more and more! This verse says that he tells his secrets to those who respect him. That's exciting! When you read the Bible and pray, you are growing your friendship with God.

• • • • • •

BEDTIME PRAYER

Dear God, Thank you for the Bible. Thank you for teaching me your ways. Help me read my Bible every day so I can know you more!

115. God Sees Your Gift

"God is fair. He will not forget the work you did and the love you showed for him by helping his people. And he will remember that you are still helping them." Hebrews 6:10

My kids and I raked the neighbors' yard. There were lots of leaves on the ground. The neighbors were older and had been sick. It was hard work. It was a big yard. We did it together. We did it for free. We did it for love. We did it to show God's love.

Showing God's love will mean that we give our time and our energy to others. It means that we put others' needs before our own. (Romans 12:10) Sometimes we might not even be thanked for our work. People may not even know it was us who gave our time, our money, or a gift. We can do it as a loving secret.

I love this verse. It reminds us of an important truth. God sees everything we do. He will remember all our work and effort. He will always remember our love.

We can work without a "thank you" from others when we remember that God knows and loves what we do.

What can you do tomorrow for someone?

• • • • •

BEDTIME PRAYER

Dear God, Please help me remember that you see all the good things I try to do.

116. Give Comfort and Strength

"So comfort each other and give each other strength, just as you are doing now." 1 Thessalonians 5:11

When I was young, I cried sometimes. I remember my cat. She would come and lay with me when I cried. It really helped me to have her near me. I felt like she understood me. She understood that I was sad. I used to talk to her. She was a comfort for me.

The Bible says that Christians should comfort each other. We can encourage - or give strength to - each other. We can listen to our friends. We can say encouraging things to our friends. And we can remind our friends about truths about God. God wants us to be like my cat! He wants us to be kind, and caring, and near to people who are sad.

Keep looking for lonely or sad friends at school. Who can you comfort? Who can you encourage?

I am praying that God will give you special friends who love him. Then those friends will be very comforting to you too!

- - - - -

BEDTIME PRAYER

Dear God, I will always remember that you comfort me. Thank you for my friend __________ who also encourages me. Please help me to do that for others!

117. Good Shepherd

"Know that the Lord is God. He made us, and we belong to him. We are his people, the sheep he tends." Psalm 100:3

There are a lot of times that the Bible talks about sheep and shepherds. I love to think about David watching the sheep. He was out in the fields by himself a lot. He wrote songs to the Lord while he watched the sheep. He protected the sheep from dangerous animals. He made sure they stayed close. He stayed there when it was sunny weather. He stayed there when it was rainy weather. He was a good shepherd.

Like David, Jesus said he is the good shepherd. He says he takes good care of his sheep. If you believe in him and follow after him, you are his sheep! Just imagine Jesus watching over you, keeping you safe, singing over you. (You can read: Zephaniah 3:17)

I like this verse! It makes me feel special. It makes me feel loved. I want you to feel that too... because you are!!

Keep this truth in your mind. He is the good shepherd. (You can read: John 10:11)

* * * * *

BEDTIME PRAYER

Dear God, Thank you for being a shepherd to me. Thank you for taking care of me. Help me to always remember your love!

118. The Gift of Love

"We love because God first loved us." 1 John 4:19

I was ten the Christmas I got the best doll ever. She had long, curly hair. She was porcelain. She had a yellow dress with little pink flowers. She had a special stand that helped her stay standing up. She had a little knob on the back. I could wind her up, and she would play a sweet little piano song. I loved her.

When I opened her on Christmas morning, I was so excited! I had always wanted such a beautiful doll. I jumped up and hugged my mom and dad. I told them, "Thank you" many times. When we get a gift, it's exciting, and we can't help but express our joy.

This verse reminds us that the reason why we love others is because God loved us. Once we "open" the gift of his love to us, we can't help but express our joy. Because he loves us, we should want to love others. It's exciting to be loved by God.

When you find someone who is kind of hard to love - or even like - remember how much God loves you. Then ask for his help to love that person with the same love.

BEDTIME PRAYER

Dear God, Thank you for loving me! I want to share your love with others! I love you!

119. Jesus' Ways

"If your enemy is hungry, feed him; if your enemy is thirsty, give him a drink." Romans 12:17-20

This verse is telling us about something super hard. It's really hard for us to not get back at someone when they wrong us. But God's ways are different than ours. This is one way that he wants us to walk in his ways.

Do you remember when Jesus was in the garden? What was he doing there? He was praying. The soldiers came to get him. His friend named Peter drew his sword. Then Peter did something shocking. He cut off the soldier's ear. Peter was ready to fight for Jesus.

Then Jesus did something even MORE shocking. He healed the soldier's ear. Then he went with the soldiers.

Jesus' ways are different than ours. It is hard to follow him sometimes. But, let's ask him for help! We can share his love by walking in his ways.

• • • • • •

BEDTIME PRAYER

Dear God, Help me to love others. Please help me to walk in your ways. I want others to know about you!

120. Tell Others!

" So go and make followers of all people in the world. Baptize them in the name of the Father and the Son and the Holy Spirit. Teach them to obey everything that I have told you. You can be sure that I will be with you always. I will continue with you until the end of the world." Matthew 28:18-20

This is the best verse to end this book on. This is Jesus' mission for all his followers. His biggest desire, his goal for us, is that we are telling others about him. He's the greatest news in the world! From his amazing, creative powers in all of creation to his rescue plan for us in our sin, there is much to tell others about!

Maybe you feel shy sometimes to talk about God. But if you keep focusing on the truths of God, they will get bigger than your fears. Tell friends and family about how great God is. Pray for them. Keep walking in Jesus' ways.

As the verse says, he will be with you always. He loves to help his children tell others about him!

● ● ● ● ● ●

BEDTIME PRAYER

Dear God, Help me talk about you to the people around me! You're so amazing! They need to know!